Enter at Your Own Risk leads you through the eight essential secrets to maximize your influence and raise a healthier, stronger child able to withstand negative cultural pressures.—Josh McDowell, author of *Evidence that Demands a Verdict*, and *Why Wait? What You Need to Know about the Teen Sexuality Crisis*

What used to absorb our interest and prayers in high school has now become the challenge of the middle school years. Patty Roth has written a book of encouragement, help, and support for those being pushed all too soon into dealing with the hostility of the secular culture.—Jay Kesler, president of Taylor University, former president of Youth for Christ, and author of *Parents and Teenagers, Emotionally Healthy Teenagers,* and a series of guides for youth groups

I would like to heartily endorse *Enter at Your Own Risk.* With a gifted amount of common sense, Patty Roth has woven together information that is extremely helpful. I especially enjoyed her "Practical Tips for Survival and Success."—Frank Minirth, M.D., author of *The Headache Book* and *The Power of Memories,* and co-author of *Happiness Is a Choice, Overcoming Depression,* and *Love Hunger*

What children are facing today in the middle school years is not what we remember from our own childhoods—or even what kids faced a decade ago. You can't expect to parent "by the seat of your pants" and make it safely through the land mines of depression, violence, sexual abuse, gangs, drugs, and suicide that threaten our impressionable children today. This book is a clarion call to all parents with children entering the middle school danger zone. In no other time in history have children needed more the security of connected families and the modeling of a strong moral value system. To make it through these years, middle schoolers must have the assurance of their parents' love and deep commitment to their welfare. This book will help you get the message across the generation gap.—Kay Kuzma, author of *In Praise of Children* and a dozen other books

In this very special book, Roth uses a delightful melange of African tales, Indiana farm stories, and adventures of her own kids to gently guide your family along the road to health. She reminds us that warmth and humor can ease us through the crises of these difficult years of parenting. Practice her tips to fuel your family soul.—Bettie B. Youngs, Ph.D., author of *Safeguarding Your Teenager from the Dragons of Life, Taste Berries for Teens,* and several other books

W9-BAC-675

CONTENTS

Foreword   9

Acknowledgments   11

Introduction   13

The Collision: Family, Culture, and the Young Teen   17

Secret #1:   *Open the Door*   32
           Understand Your Middle Schooler's World

Secret #2:   *Walk Carefully*   47
           Balance Support and Control

Secret #3:   *Always Knock First*   64
           Maintain Firm, Flexible Boundaries

Secret #4:   *Turn Down the Heat*   77
           Use Negotiation to Resolve Conflict

Secret #5:   *Share Power*   96
           Show Respect and Give Freedom

Secret #6:   *Match Your Walk and Your Talk*   108
           Live Your Spiritual Values

Secret #7:   *Pull Up a Chair*   121
           Establish Connection through Warmth
           and Affection

Secret #8:   *Step Back*   135
           Encourage Autonomy

Tie It All Together: Supporting Middle Schoolers in Their   149
           Search for Identity

Appendix 1:   Substance Abuse   157

Appendix 2:   Stepfamily Stages of Adjustment   163

Appendix 3:   Adolescents and Suicide   168

Appendix 4:   Adolescents Involved in Satanism   171

Appendix 5:   Adolescents and Eating Disorders   174

Notes   178

Bibliography   184

Subject Index   191

FOREWORD

As a Christian psychiatrist, I have said for over twenty-five years that the toughest years in most people's lives are those from age twelve to age sixteen. Those early middle school years are particularly difficult, because as an eleven- or twelve-year-old you're a little boy or a little girl, but by the time you're sixteen, you're an adult man or adult woman. The changes that take place during that transition can result in great turmoil.

I have also said that if you took a normal thirteen-year-old and considered him an adult, he would probably be deemed mentally ill because a thirteen-year-old's thought patterns are so different from those of an adult. As a father of six children who are now all in their twenties, I remember those middle school years very well. The child knew everything; I knew nothing. Yet together, with a lot of TLC, we worked our way through those years successfully.

Filled with good practical principles, *Enter at Your Own Risk* is an excellent tool that every parent of a middle school child should have to guide their children through those "impossible" years.

The book offers practical, biblical advice, humor, and a great deal of wisdom from Roth's experience as a therapist. She covers a wide range of helpful topics such as boundaries, teen sex, and how to encourage teen autonomy, with many tips for survival and success.

I highly recommend this book. In fact, it should be required reading for every parent of a middle schooler.

Paul Meier, M.D.
Cofounder and Medical Director of the New Life Clinics with over 450 therapists in 103 clinics throughout the U.S. and Canada

ACKNOWLEDGMENTS

My thanks go to the unnamed families I have worked with, for their lives, their stories, and the dignity they exhibited in desiring to change. To my editor, Joan Guest, for her thorough and consistent push to improve. To the scores of parents and their children who attended my workshops and gave valuable feedback.

To those who consented to being interviewed at length, for their wisdom and insights: Principal Lance Otis, Youth Pastor Steve Inrig, Ashley and Allison Moreland, Daniel and Ruth Issler, Donald Tavie, Principal Jim Kissinger, Vice-Principal Judy Kissinger, Vice-Principal Linda Kewin, Sergeant Charlie Wilhite, Don Couchman, Michèle and Kristopher Roth and many of their friends. Thanks to Howard Ostendorff for his story and to Greg Evans for his kind permission to use "Luann."

To my special Monday night support group and their kids for their prayers and encouragement: Barry and Lynn Martin, Walt and Joyce DeBlauw, Bob and Wanda Welles, Odo and Bev Siahaya, Edie and Bob Gordon, Karlene Stehling, Cheri Tucci, and Ray Wingert.

To my writing group: Ed Elmendorff and Robert Boehm, for their warm encouragement and invaluable critique of my manuscript.

To old friends Klaus and Beth Issler, J. P. and Hope Moreland, Greg and Debbie Kappas, and Keith Shubert, who supported me early on in the process.

To my parents, Porter and Esther Davis, who believed in me, my sisters and brother and their families for being my connection: Judy and Dan Montgomery, Marta and John Webster, and Steve and Debbie Davis.

And most of all, my thanks go to Bill, my husband, for his encouragement, affirmation, and belief in me; to my children,

Michèle and Kristopher, who by their lives are the best endorsements I could ever have with their wisdom, playfulness, and strong character. A special thanks to Michèle for her extra work in typing and retyping the manuscript when the floppy disk inexplicably corrupted beyond repair.

INTRODUCTION

As my daughter, Michèle, walked away from her last class in middle school, I proposed that she and I write a book together to help parents understand junior high kids (as middle schoolers were called at that time). Her first response: "But, Mom, no one can understand a junior higher!"

We looked at the piles of notes written back and forth between friends, a collection that she still had stashed under her bed, and realized that writing about friends at that time would be just too personal and invasive. So the project was delayed.

A few years later, I began the research and the interviewing. By then I had been to scores of basketball, soccer, and volleyball practices and games, mother-daughter Ticktocker (National Charity League) events, shopping trips, and field trips; I had hosted birthday parties, invited tens of young teens over for dinner, supervised groups playing basketball with the two hoops in front of our house, and commiserated with many parents. In addition, my practice as a family therapist continued to reveal the seriousness of the struggles faced by parents new to the task. Speaking invitations flowed in from middle school parent groups, YWCA groups, and church groups. Parents wanted help for these tricky years.

Voices from the academic world as well as from observers of popular culture pointed out the risks middle schoolers face. In her book *Reviving Ophelia,* Dr. Mary Pipher sounded a warning call for parents to wake up to what our culture is doing to the self-esteem of young teen girls. Others acknowledged that young teen boys suffer a hit to esteem as well. Major universities produced research demonstrating how vulnerable adolescents are to alcohol and drug use during the middle school years. Cigarette companies targeted middle schools with their billboard campaigns. Creative vodka ads became hot items for young teens to collect. Worse yet, parents in their busyness abdicated to this culture and peer pressure.

Despite these alarm bells, research, interviews, my private practice work with families, and discussions with friends have led me to the same conclusion: The family can still make a difference, a very big difference. A middle schooler's problem behaviors are frequently a signal to alert the family that it's time to change. Old family habits may be keeping a family blind and stuck, fated to repeat patterns that will again and again produce problems during this new developmental stage of the young teen. When the family learns to respond correctly, the middle schooler can adjust well and mature, and the family can move on.

Not a how-to-build-a-safe-fortress book, *Enter at Your Own Risk* is a fitness center book for families. Parents with a fortress mentality, as friend and educator Marsha Bunnell terms it, end up with kids with a weak infrastructure. When I think of a fortress, I picture the thick walls of the square solid fort perched atop a hill in Ankara, Turkey, erected for protection and defense against attacking foes. Parents with a fortress mentality erect walls of resistance against a corrupt world out to get their children. In so doing, they isolate them and eclipse opportunities for building strength. Their children's strength is confined to their fortress alone. Like natives in an isolated culture, such teens will succumb to the outside world when the fortress falls, since they have had no opportunities to develop their own boundaries.

Smart parents build the infrastructure of character instead. A child's inner sense of self and strength of character are like moral and emotional bones and muscles. Bones and muscles need exercise to grow, weight-bearing exercise to strengthen. Just as feet need to pound pavement, arms need to throw baseballs, and fingers need to grasp and manipulate solid objects, so a child's character needs strength training in a real world. Kids with this kind of infrastructure make good choices on their own. Their immunity lies in their strong thinking that comes from grappling with real life in a fitness center family.

This book approaches parenting from the perspective of psychotherapy called family systems. The opening section focuses on the head-on collision of family, culture, and the middle schooler. The eight essential secrets to a family's success follow. Chapter nine ties it all together with ways parents can contribute to their young teen's strong identity. Appendices are devoted to five special topics—substance abuse, divorce and stepfamilies, suicidal feelings, dabbling in satanism, and eating disorders. As the world of your middle schooler enlarges, she and you will be confronted with people facing these issues.

The cases described in this book are composites of true stories. They have been deliberately scrambled in order to protect my clients' rights to privacy and confidentiality. The interviews are credited to the actual people interviewed.

THE COLLISION:
FAMILY, CULTURE,
AND THE YOUNG
TEEN

P robably every reader of this book knows of a family that, after functioning well for years, becomes seriously unbalanced when a middle-school-age child shocks everyone with delinquent or unusual behavior. Such a family may be getting a strong hint that their way of relating to each other needs to change. They need to make a course correction.

Hailey, twelve, stole candy to save her family. Blinded by family patterns, her parents had had no earlier warning that they were on a crash course. Lucky for all of them, the security guard caught Hailey.

Hailey's mother brought her to my office, commenting, "I don't get it. She had four quarters in her pocket. The candy cost sixty-five cents."

Hailey had the usual complaints: "Mom doesn't ever buy the right food [meaning not enough chips, Cokes, and Twinkies]. My parents nag us too much about our chores. I don't like my mom. She favors my younger sister. *My parents are always too busy.*"

None of these complaints explained why Hailey stole something she could easily afford. But her shoplifting hit the family like a wrecking ball. Her parents stopped in their tracks, trying to figure out what was wrong. Her mother took time off from work to pick her up at school and bring her into my office. Her father dropped his extra commitments at work. He turned committees over to a colleague. He gave up coaching the boys' roller blade hockey team at a local hockey arena. These changes freed him to be home with Hailey and her two sisters after school so he could supervise them and their friends, hoping to prevent another run-in with the law for Hailey.

Did Hailey consciously plan out this strategy to force her parents to be home more? No. But her cry for help resulted in the temporary solution of one of her biggest complaints: "My parents are too busy for us." Hailey was angry, resentful, and depressed. She subconsciously chose an action whose resolution would solve her problem.

A month later, her parents, thinking all was well, returned to their prior hectic routines. This time, Hailey's fourteen-year-old sister, Christi, sounded the alarm. Her algebra teacher called her parents with suspicions of a drug problem, and her closest friend called, saying that Christi was going to kill herself.

Over time, as trust was built, the family story unfolded. Larry, the father, had married young. His first wife, Saranda, was seventeen and pregnant at the time. They quickly had three more children, one stillborn. But Saranda lamented her lost childhood and wanted her adolescence back. She left the family, divorced Larry, and moved to Mexico.

Four years later, Saranda unexpectedly called saying she wanted to see the kids. Larry, although skeptical, packed their bags for a visit. He hoped with desperation that she had changed and that her mothering instinct had overtaken her bent towards irresponsibility and impulsiveness. But it was not to be so. Hailey remembered spending the first few days of this visit with her mother and on the fifth evening baking cookies while her mother went out with friends. That night, Saranda drank too much and, in a trancelike state, ran her car off the road into a telephone pole, dying immediately.

Larry, in the best way he knew possible, tried to pick up the pieces. He wanted to cheer the children up, so he decided never to discuss the accident and their mother with them again. He also decided he would not tell them other tragic family history. Hailey knew few of these details. Her father had skillfully avoided any discussions about her mother up to that point. When the subject came up, he told only sketches of the reality. Christi knew even less than Hailey, as she kept to herself and did not ask any questions.

During the year that Hailey came in to my office, Larry was gradually convinced to gently talk with his older daughter. He asked Christi if she had ever wondered why she had straight hair when the rest of his children had curly hair like his. He asked if Christi had ever wondered why her skin was darker than everyone else's. Of course Christi had noticed many times how different she was, but she had never wanted to ask, thinking the question might upset her father. Still, she had wondered, and she felt like she didn't belong to the family.

Larry then bluntly told his daughter that she was not his biological child—that Christi's mother was married before, and that her first husband looked remarkably like Christi. Christi's response of "Oh cool!" falsely reassured Larry of the relative unimportance of this biological data to her.

In fact, this information was startling and shocking to Christi. It felt right. It confirmed her inner suspicions, giving her a sense of momentary relief from the tensions in her soul. But it also opened up new fears and strong emotions in her:

> *What if Dad didn't really want me? Who is my biological father, and why did he ditch my mother? Was he a useless bum? Am I one too? This information belonged to me. Why didn't anyone ever tell me about him??! Probably because I'm just a charity case, and when they get tired of taking care of me, they'll get rid of me. Maybe I should just help them along. I'll give them a reason to like me even less. Or maybe I'll just let myself die like my mother did.*

Hailey's shoplifting had little to do with a lack of money. Christi's drug use and threats of suicide had little to do with liking drugs or wanting to die. These behaviors had a lot to do with confused feelings and deep needs which emanated from a history that had been erased. The girls' actions were screams to the family that this family needed to make some changes or they could die inside.

Larry's family was willing to do what was necessary. Susan, his wife of five years, agreed radical change was needed, and they decided that a parent fully available at home was important for these children struggling with feelings of abandonment and a diffuse sense of belonging. Although change this drastic is not always necessary, this family as a group decided to move to a southern state where the cost of living was low enough that they could survive on Susan's salary alone. There they set up a weekly family meeting to talk about how each person was feeling as they continued to explore how their family background had influenced them. They began to feel more connected, regardless of biological parentage. The family meeting helped them to anticipate problem areas as well as point the way to probable solutions. They grew in their abilities to meet each other's needs. This family made the course correction required for all of them to grow in a healthy way as individuals and as a group.

WHAT MIDDLE SCHOOLERS AND COWS HAVE IN COMMON

Back on the farm in Indiana where I was visiting my parents with our children, I observed a phenomenon that happens in *families,* or herds, of cattle that have been living together, a phenomenon with parallels to the experience of Hailey's family. One hazy morning at 5:30, I was abruptly awakened by two loud sounds. One was the braying of a large group of cattle; they sounded as if they were plaintively beseeching our help. The other was the sound of our son, Kristopher, calling for Grandpa to get up, as a cow was loose in the front yard (quite a sight for a California kid!). We all jumped into our clothes and ran outside to corral the pesky heifer. After cajoling and blocking, and letting Smoky the English shepherd do his job, we saw the runaway safely back with the others in the field.

Indoors, sipping coffee and munching breakfast breads, I asked my dad how the cow had gotten loose. He half chuckled as he explained he didn't know how the cow had gotten loose, but he knew why. "This happens every year," he explained. "It's past springtime, and it's been time to move the cattle to the pasture out by the woods for a couple of weeks. They've eaten most of what is nutritious in this field, and they get pretty restless until we move them to the other pasture. It's as if the herd gets together and sends one of the heifers out of the field. Then the rest of the herd gather together in the corner like they did this morning and start loudly bawling at the heifer on the loose. That's what you heard at 5:30 A.M. It's their way of letting me know they're ready to move on to another pasture, one that has more plentiful growth they can graze on. I don't know how that heifer got out. Steve [my brother] and I went all the way around the fence, and we couldn't find any holes she could have squeezed through. But somehow she got out."

I thought about that noisy intrusion on the usually quiet farm and marveled that even a group of cows can figure out that their needs are not being met and that they need to create a ruckus to get the attention of the one who can make the necessary changes. Similarly, in a family changing developmental stages, if new needs go unmet, the stress can focus on one member who *acts out* in uncharacteristic ways to force attention to the problem. The good news is that these cryptic family messages can be deciphered and the needed changes can be made, if the family has some degree of flexibility and closeness.

A family is like a mobile made of objects with different sizes and shapes suspended from the ceiling, all interconnected. Pull one shape of the mobile and the others all move. Let it go and the mobile erratically dances until it rediscovers its equilibrium.

When a child enters the middle school years, the family mobile is especially affected. Adolescence has been called a "time of normal psychosis" by Frank Pittman, Atlanta therapist and author.[1] Think of a wind spinning through that mobile; the pieces scatter and flit about in all directions until they fall to rest and some organization appears again. In the same way, when a well-functioning family with elementary-school-age children is hit with the whirlwind of adolescence, the family will be shaken up and must change as a result of the encounter. My husband remains convinced that on the first day of seventh grade the hormones turn on and the brain turns off, with family life never to be the same again.

THE CHALLENGE OF TODAY'S CULTURE

The family mobile is suspended today in a world very different from the world of our youth and from the world of our grandparents' youth. Author Mary Pipher describes the oppression our teens live under as a "dangerous, sexualized, media-saturated culture."[2] Researchers from Indiana University released shocking evidence of a thirty-six-month window of increased vulnerability in a child's life when his risk of starting to use drugs and alcohol is dramatically increased.[3] This window starts at the end of sixth grade and closes at the end of ninth grade. During this window of vulnerability, one-half of cigarette and alcohol use begins. More staggering is the news that over two-thirds of continuing marijuana use starts during this time period, and three-fourths of pill abuse (stimulants, depressants, and narcotics) starts during these thirty-six months. Today, the ages twelve through fourteen are truly the risky years.

Think of some of the changes in our culture from the time when parents of current teenagers were teens themselves. In 1972, hand-held calculators hit the market. In 1982 the *New York Times* reported on a mysterious new disease, AIDS. Dr. Harvey Elder, Chief of Infectious Diseases at Loma Linda University Medical Center, saw his first AIDS patient that year and speculated that he might see one or two of these patients in his lifetime. In 1985, Rock Hudson died of AIDS, crack cocaine appeared, and Madonna sang about our "material world" and called herself "a material girl." In 1989 the USSR held open elections, East Germany opened the Berlin Wall, and *The Simpsons* debuted on TV.

When I was an eighth grader riding the school bus and a high school boy tried cutting my hair with his knife, I turned around and socked him in the nose. The bus driver laughed. Today, a middle schooler could be charged with assault or, worse yet, could be stabbed. In 1991, the number of fifteen- to nineteen-year-olds killed was more than double the total in 1985. In 1992 and 1993, Polly Klaas was kidnapped and murdered, and the TV show *Beavis and*

Butthead debuted. In 1997, violence hit closer to home when the 18-year-old sister of one of my son's friends was murdered with a gunshot while riding one afternoon in a car with her boyfriend.

Webster's New World Dictionary now includes the following, reflecting further culture changes: *cyberspace, Chechnya, blended family, biscotti, criminalist, dis* ("to show disrespect to," originally Black English), *European Union, Generation X, in-your-face* (a hyphenated adjective), *Prozac, hanta virus, twelve step, and trophy wife.*

The emotional punch of these gargantuan changes in our culture hits the family mobile with a force often difficult to counterbalance or repel, especially since so many of the changes affect our children's everyday lives. Drugs and weapons are now available in the same blocks as middle schools and, in some cases, elementary schools. In some middle schools, chlamydia is now a serious problem, as the median age of the students' first sexual intercourse is thirteen-and-a-half for girls and twelve-and-a-half for boys.[4] I get calls from parents who are frantic about discovering their teens awake at three in the morning looking at pornography on the Internet. Such dramatic risks leave us all hoping that we have forged resilient connections in our family mobiles.

FAMILY HISTORY REPEATS ITSELF

Both current family research and the ancient teachings of the Old Testament (including Deuteronomy 6:1-3 and Exodus 20:4-6) tell us that patterns may be passed on in our families for generations. Even young children seem to understand this. One of ours asked one day, "Mom and Dad, when you were little, did your parents make you go to bed early and keep rules and stuff?" When we responded yes, he continued, "Then are you just trying to do to us what they did to you?"

These family patterns evolve in a variety of ways. Since all parents have grown up in a family themselves and since no one is perfect, all parents will carry some unresolved emotional issues from their imperfect parents. (Someone has suggested that a new group be started in the style of Adult Children of Alcoholics and Adult Children of a Dysfunctional Family groups—one that deals with the problems suffered as Adult Children of Parents). A woman who has always felt indebted to her own mother for all the sacrifices she made for her might marry a man who is angry at his parents and wants to owe no one anything. An issue such as this often resurfaces when an oldest child reaches middle school age, and the carryover of disappointment and resentment can weigh heavily on these sensitive young teens.

This begins to sound as though we should be able to blame our great-grandparents for any problems we are having today with our young teens; yet the two groups never met each other. Blame is, in fact, not the issue. Understanding and change are the issues. Alice Miller talked about this when she wrote, "Infectious diseases need not spread if the virus is known."[5] Knowing, understanding, and taking responsibility for our part in idiosyncratic family viruses gives us the freedom to change as well as the ability to better parent and protect our children. I was dramatically reminded of this principle when I heard the following story several years ago from two missionary pilots. The setting was Zaire, West Africa.

One warm day, several friends went swimming upstream at their favorite swimming hole, a location they had frequented for twelve years. The two pilots and two other families took inner tubes to play in the river. On this particular day, unbeknownst to the group, hidden in the murky water at the bottom of the river was a mama hippo and her baby. Contrary to the popular yet distorted view of hippos as harmless, plodding animals, African hippos are ferocious animals of lightning-quick speed. Their huge mouths enclose two large, tusklike teeth, and mothers are very protective of their babies.

While this group was playing on the surface of the river, a movement disturbed the mama hippo and she surfaced, wildly chomping. The men frantically tried to get all of the children out of the river. After much struggle and wrestling to pull one girl's foot from the hippo's mouth, all the children were rescued.

Looking back at this horrifying incident, it is easy to see that if they had known the hippos were there, the group would have made different choices. They could have remained on the banks of the river. They could have found a different location to swim. Perhaps they could have even hired some hippo experts to chase the hippos away. These options would all have kept them safe. But they were working without full information, and the attack was even more surprising because they had never expected hippos to frequent this familiar location.

Communicating with middle schoolers can also hide the possibility of deadly encounters. A seemingly innocent encounter dealing with familiar topics can escalate into a shocking attack when unexpressed issues emerge suddenly like the hippos. These old issues could include the secret of a mother's teen pregnancy brought to mind when her adolescent daughter begins to talk about boys, or a father's experience of sexual abuse as a young teen brought back to him when his son becomes a teenager and wants more freedom. A father whose son returns home at 8:36 P.M. instead of 8:30 might be affected by a relationship with his own father, who would rage at the slightest infraction of a rule. A mother who repeatedly saw her father punch and throw her mother across the room might now react as she watches her husband's anger rise when their daughter is late coming to the dinner table.

These old issues, hidden as secrets, limit your ways of seeing your children. Lurking just under the surface, they can easily trigger old reactions to new situations, repetitions of old patterns rather than thoughtful, creative responses you choose based on the current people and circumstances.

RETURNING TO THE PAST TO GO FORWARD

A family I worked with several years ago struggled with the fact that their oldest child, just entering middle school, would grab kitchen knives and threaten to kill herself whenever she was frustrated. They were a loving family, yet nothing they tried eliminated this behavior. When the mother began to study their family backgrounds, she discovered that three generations back in her family, there had been two violent deaths and six suicides, along with a history of violence on her husband's side as well. Knowing this, she and her husband began to search for clues as to how this pattern was being unwittingly passed on. They noticed things that they themselves did that could be contributing to the problem. They found several slang expressions, as well as nonverbal gestures, they used regularly that had to do with killing and violence, although they had used them affectionately ("Slay you with kindness," "I could just kill you with love," "That'll be the death of you"). As they persistently replaced these linguistic patterns with nurturing phrases minus any reference to violence or death, their daughter also began to change.

People in Ghana have an Akan word that could be used to describe this process of understanding the past to change the future: *Sankofa,* which means "returning to the past to go forward."

Oddly enough, a family's unique yet destructive patterns often have grown out of an intentionally constructive beginning. David and Esther, for example, tried to make meals together a satisfying family time for their children and young teen, but such times were a disaster. As a father, David wanted meals to be a time to connect with the kids and monitor their eating habits. Esther reacted negatively to his suggestions and to her kids' complaints. Bickering and criticism would take over and then Esther would coldly withdraw and leave the table. Gradually, each person began to eat alone.

In studying her background, Esther realized the importance food had in her family as she grew up. Both Esther's mother and father were survivors of the Holocaust with vivid memories of the dead and dying. They remembered how those in the camps with a few extra pounds lived a few more days. To them, the freedom to eat extra was an opportunity to be grasped, and this attitude was fueled by an urgency to protect and preserve life. Esther, however, as a young teen, was concerned about her appearance and did not want to gain weight. Fiery arguments would erupt between her and her parents, always over the issue of food and mealtimes. She became conditioned to react to any set expectations of others, including her own children, about meals.

Unraveling the origins of this mystery allowed Esther to look at mealtimes in a fresh way and to experiment with different options. She and David found that they could take turns with being in charge of the meal; they could eat in different locations, sometimes spreading a blanket on the floor, sometimes using candlelight and china.

As they introduced flexibility into their mealtimes, Esther's anxiety was alleviated, and the children loved the new approach.

THE FAMILY IS THE ANSWER

Our homes are assaulted on a daily basis by what is going on in our culture and by family patterns we may not even recognize. But lives and history can change when families begin to realize their own resourcefulness, understand their own family patterns, and make healthy changes.

Contrary to popular opinion, the latest research informs us that the family does have the primary influence on young teens.[6] This is not to discount the influence of peers but rather to focus on what a family *can* do both to build strong relationships and to face a crisis if it should arise. What can families do? First, they can take a look at the characteristics and actions of strong, healthy families who know the eight secrets we will be discussing. Then, if they are facing a problem such as a middle school child who abuses substances, runs away, or exhibits defiance, they can acknowledge the immediate problem, look at the family structure to see if it is one that no longer meets the needs of everyone, and make any changes (sometimes simple, but not necessarily easy) that are required.

IT PAYS TO PREPARE

The middle school years bring a new culture into the home, and parents who are unprepared for this may find themselves making crucial mistakes. Tannen tells the true story of a woman who, unprepared for a culture she was visiting, met up with serious danger.[7] This polite American woman started out on a cruise but ended up in a Turkish jail.

While exploring some ruins alone, she encountered a persistent Turkish peddler who was selling artifacts illegal for her to buy. She did not wish to offend him but did not communicate her lack of interest effectively. In fact, out of her ignorance of the Turkish culture, this tourist unwittingly gave the peddler the opposite impression. Everything she did was an accepted signal in the Turkish culture to indicate a willingness to bargain—her being alone, looking directly at the man, handling the artifacts, listening to him, and offering a lower price all signaled the peddler to persist. Any Turkish woman would have known that all she needed to do was to take the artifacts, place them on the ground, and walk away.

The tourist ended up buying some artifacts so the peddler would leave her alone. Her view of politeness combined with her American worldview kept her from understanding that she was communicating something very different from what she intended. As a result, when she returned to the ship, she was arrested by customs officials and thrown in jail. The cost of her ignorance was high.

When my husband and I went to Turkey, we benefited from the woman's story. We noticed that as long as we related as friendly, polite Americans, we had vendors tagging along with us, trying to sell us something. Once we made the switch to thinking and acting like Turkish nationals, the vendors did not even try. When one particularly pesky girl placed her items for sale on my arm, I simply took them off and placed them on the ground and continued walking. Without flinching she picked them up and went off to look for another tourist.

You can benefit from this woman's story as well. Choosing to understand and respect your young teen's worldview can save you from paying a potentially high price for ignorance. By doing all you can to learn about middle schoolers in general and your child in particular, you can prepare your family for a safer and more successful journey through these years.

PRACTICE TIPS FOR SURVIVAL AND SUCCESS

1. To learn more about your intergenerational family patterns, try interviewing family members. Learning their perspectives can help you identify family themes, bring secrets out in the open when necessary, and understand your unique family system. Then it will be easier to implement healthy changes.

   Interview grandparents on both sides of the family. Interview great-aunts and great-uncles, cousins, and other relatives. If grandparents and other older relatives have died, try to find people who knew them well. Ask them what they remember about older members of the family. If possible, use a video camera or a tape recorder to make records of your personal family history. Get the entire family involved; even young children can ask questions. Your middle schooler can interview *you,* the parent, or aunts and uncles with similar questions. Here are some questions to start you off:

- How did you get to school?
- What did you do after school?
- What were your chores like?
- Where was the center of warmth in your home when you were between six and ten years old?
- How did you celebrate Christmas? Birthdays? Thanksgiving?
- Describe your mother.
- Describe your father.
- What was your favorite thing to do when you were a teenager?
- How did you meet Grandpa (or whoever is the spouse)?
- What advice did your parents give you about marriage?
- What adjectives would you use to describe my mom/dad when she/he was a child?
- What words of wisdom would you want to pass on to your grandchildren?
- Which of the following things were/are most important in our family?

Education	Having a relationship with God
Learning a skill	Being on time
Family relationships	Thinking positively
Keeping a clean house	Being creative
Expressing anger	Being neat
Avoiding anger	Being skeptical
Being polite	Being a leader
Privacy	Being a good neighbor
Joking around	Making a good impression
Being serious	Thinking for yourself
Going to church	Sports

2. Take a look at your family patterns. Identify areas where your family may need to refocus and move in a healthier direction. This step may be easier after reading the rest of the book.

   Here is one example: Mom's family never expressed anger openly. People stayed calm and no feathers were ruffled. However, no one would know what bothered anyone else, and toes were always stepped on. Dad's family, meanwhile, expressed anger in a volatile way. Family members always knew what you thought, and you could get things off your chest. However, family members sometimes were afraid to talk to each other, and it was easy to degenerate from discussion into name calling. Sometimes the sensitive ones felt crushed.

   How can the family in this example begin to refocus? As a first step, come up with a one-line principle about anger to use. Possibilities:

   - It is okay to say you are angry, but it is not okay to hurt someone.
   - Tell the truth about feelings with a caring attitude.

   What pattern characterizes your family? Can you state a healthy principle that would help? Talk about this new principle with your family. Begin to practice it.

3. As you discover family secrets, decide to gently and kindly talk about them with the family members, as it is age-appropriate. Discuss how these secrets may have affected your family.

4. To better prepare your young teen to cope with the rapidly changing world of today, teach your young teen to *think* about marketing. Television commercials and magazine advertisements are trying to sell products by appealing to your wants and needs. Watch some TV commercials together and discuss them using questions such as the following:

   - Is it well done?
   - What are they selling?

- What are they saying about it?
- What are they saying it will do for you?
- Is it true?
- What are the values they are trying to impart?

You might see a commercial for a certain brand of jeans, one which implies that the jeans will fit so well that you will look wonderful. If you buy these jeans, you will be popular and sexy and have a lot of older boyfriends. Of course this is not true. This commercial displays the values that happiness is based on how you look and what you wear and that acceptance depends on material things.

In another commercial the cartoon characters that advertise cigarettes may be well done, showing excellent design and a high level of creativity. The cigarettes they are selling are depicted as a normal part of everyday life. The commercial may imply that smoking these cigarettes would give you a cool image—the image of someone who is sophisticated and attractive to others. Again, this is not true. The implied values: Self-esteem and feeling comfortable with yourself come from things you can buy. It is okay to do harmful things to your body if you enjoy them and they make you look good.

After discussing the questions about marketing, talk together as a family about what values are true and healthy for your family. Here are some possibilities:

- Who you are as a person is more important than what you own.
- To feel accepted by others, you must first accept yourself.
- Our bodies are valuable and need to be cared for.
- Happiness is a byproduct of living your life based on principles.

Try this same process with a video, movie, or TV show. Together as a family, watch a movie about teens, for instance. Discuss it using some of the suggested questions above. Encouraging your young teen to question and think about what she sees will help develop her character infrastructure.

1
SECRET #1:
OPEN THE DOOR
UNDERSTAND YOUR MIDDLE SCHOOLER'S WORLD

Student doctors in America learn the rule, When you hear hoof beats, think horses. Physician Melinda Skau, working in Nigeria, comments, "That doesn't work in Africa!"—a continent where zebras outnumber horses. In the same way, middle school and the teenage years are like another culture, and we as adults have to broaden our perspective in order to understand the teens with whom we relate.

When my husband and I lived in France, we learned early on the importance of understanding worldviews. We were studying French in a small village and we found that cultural differences flourished—from foods we ate (blood sausage, considered a delicacy), to how we ate (hot milk and coffee in a large bowl for breakfast), to when we ate, to always greeting friends with kisses (one on each cheek or at least in that direction). There were government differences too. Strikes were a part of French life. Once the postal system went on strike for six weeks; we got no mail, and no one seemed to want to do anything about it. Sometimes I longed for the predictability and stability of the United States. The differences that at first had seemed exciting eventually became annoying. Our way would have been simpler and more efficient, or so we thought.

As we began speaking French more fluently, we were encouraged but still felt something was missing. That necessary connection between people seemed to elude us. Then one day a French friend and her British husband invited us to visit them. We spent the entire day learning about the French—what they value, how they see life, and what's important to them. We learned that while American families prioritize a home and cars in their budgets, French families spend most of their budget on food and vacation. While Americans like to be direct in making a point in a conversation, a Frenchman may talk about everything except the main point, thus indirectly highlighting his view.

Feeling better informed, we returned to our home in Lyon and began our work again. French friends and colleagues began to tell us our French had improved. Our diction and intonation had not changed, however, and our vocabularies could not have increased that rapidly. What had changed was our *understanding*. We now understood more about the French *worldview*—how they saw the world. With our understanding came a new respect for and sensitivity to the French, which changed how we related to them and, in response, how they perceived us. We relaxed, and communication improved.

THE WORLDVIEW OF A YOUNG TEEN—YOUR KEY TO CONNECTION

Your middle schooler has emerged with a different worldview and values, new factors you may not recognize. His hormones have begun to kick in. His body has started changing its shape. He no longer identifies with young children or with you. If he did not go through the terrible twos as a toddler, he may likely go through them now (which is better for you—saving them for the early twenties is worse). One of our friends says her daughter went through this rebellious stage at age two and again as a young teen.

The key to minimizing such a rebellion does not lie with the child, but with the parent! It is the parent who must learn a lesson about how to relate differently to this emerging self. You can choose to ignore the new worldview just as you might choose to ignore a soaring temperature gauge in a car, or to denigrate it, but if building a relationship is part of your goal, you need to respect it.

One of the most important changes in your middle schooler is the boost in significance of her relationships with peers. Her ability to fit in is crucial. As thirteen-year-old Ruth explained to me, "having friends" is the most important thing in middle school. Lance Otis, who retired in 1996 from his position as principal of Colton Middle School in California, explained:

> They have such tender little hearts. They easily change. They'll have a deep friend now, and if their friend doesn't do something exactly right, it's gone. They've gone to somebody else. Many of them are very insecure, fearful at times. I think they're frightened. . . .
>
> Parents need to understand that these kids, from one moment to another, are focusing on a hundred things. They're terribly concerned about how they look, terribly concerned about who likes them, terribly concerned about rumors— what somebody said that somebody said that somebody said that has absolutely no validity at all.

His observations match up with this note written from one seventh grader to another:

> Hi! I'm sorry this is so messy—I don't have any paper. Could you do me a big favor? Will you find you-know-who's schedule (not John). I don't want anybody to know I like you-know-who (X.X.) or John, ok? All the nail polish on my pinkies came off. Cheap stuff she gave me. I hate *Karin*. In PE I got goose bumps on my legs *all* over so she said I had chicken legs and she said I have a *beak* nose. Sad, huh? She said she was just kidding, but I could have said something about her fat if I wanted to but I didn't. Mr. Griffin is having a cow about us being conceited *again*. He's comparing us with Japan. Well, guess I better go—we have the same lunch (duh!) and I hope Karin doesn't eat with us!
>
> L.Y.L.A.S. ["Love you like a sis"]

Researchers tell us what parents already know—young teens become more self-centered. (One parent said, "They become leeches.") They become aware of their sexuality; they become more aggressive; and they need to become more independent. They want parents to take care of them and to leave them alone at the same time. In the words of parents, young teens become more moody, critical, flighty, sarcastic, anxious, confused, rebellious, angry, and volatile. Ruth, at thirteen, said that what was hardest for her parents was attitude: "They think we [her older brother and she] got sassier, more disobedient, more stubborn . . . And," she added softly, "we probably did."

Because your young teen is rethinking what you have taught her, her *inside* is not so solid; her basic sense of self has not firmed up and she feels a greater need for her *outside* to be okay—looking good on the outside becomes a way to make the inside feel better. "These kids are coming into the school with a high degree of uncertainty of who they are," said Principal Otis. Of course, you do not want your teen to stay this way for life, and he will not if you give him the space, understanding, warmth, and guidance he needs. It might mean letting him wear a T-shirt and jeans like most other boys to the after-school Valentine's dance, even though all of the girls are wearing dressy outfits, and few of the kids actually do any dancing. Once our son even worked and saved his money to rent a tuxedo jacket to wear with his jeans and hightop athletic shoes to his middle school dance.

Your teen's effort to keep her outside looking good may extend to her experimentation with the rhythm and lingo of friends from a different ethnic group. She may even begin to sound just like one of her closest friends—same words, same intonations. Your child's hair style and how it looks each morning becomes an item of utmost importance. I can remember myself at age thirteen thinking I would never live through the days until my hair grew out from a too-closely-cropped haircut.

Expressions you thought you understood now mean something else to your middle schooler. *Bad,* for example, switched to meaning "really good" years ago. I also remember my shock and readiness to impose restrictions when Michèle told us she was "going out" with a boy she knew at church. Then I discovered that that meant they would say Hi to each other and might possibly sit together at the youth group meetings.

Greg Evans, cartoonist of "Luann," illustrates the worldview of the middle schooler well in "A Poem by Luann DeGroot":

> How to kiss and How to stop, What to wear and where to shop,
> How to make my hair look better, How to fill out my new sweater,
> What to say when He walks by, what to do to catch his eye,
> How to act, how to be, how to make the best of me,
> Where to go and where to turn-*THESE* are things I need to learn!
> But, Here I sit all day in school, Learning math and grammar rules."[1]

To communicate in a way that makes a connection with a young teen, you must understand that he is in transition. Young teens are no longer little children, with childlike ways of seeing the world. Neither are they adults, or even older teenagers. As Steve Inrig, youth pastor for middle school students at Trinity Evangelical Free Church of Redlands, California, says, "They're starting to emerge as adults. I think the number one thing is just trying to figure out who they are, understanding where they fit in their social group, defining who they are in their family, what kind of music they listen to, what kind of clothes they wear. Those things are so much attached to their whole identity."

THE MIDDLE SCHOOL TRANSITION

So what exactly does the young teen move out of and what does he move into? What he is leaving is the important world of childhood. Erikson lists four developmental tasks as necessary to circumnavigate during the childhood years:[2]

- From birth to one and a half years: to develop a sense of *basic trust*, in contrast to a sense of pervasive mistrust

■ From one and a half years to three years: to develop a sense of *autonomy* or separateness from Mother, and hence not be burdened by a sense of shame and self-doubt

■ From three years to six years: to develop a sense of *initiative*, not guilt

■ From six years to twelve years: to develop the ability to be *industrious*.

During these four stages of development in childhood, imagination and play are paramount. Pretending is the way your child tries out new behaviors and desires without risk in a healthy family. Whether trying on Mother's old formal or dressing up a doll in doll-sized evening dress, a child can imagine and play in the total safety of her parents' protective supervision.

Then, the hormones arrive, the mind jumps to abstract reasoning capabilities, the body changes, and your young teen clamors to *experience* what she had only imagined before. "Firsts" characterize this new period of adolescence, and with each new first experience comes another depth of emotion not felt before.[3] Older and wiser Kris (twenty-three) now says that middle school kids do not want to learn from your experiences: "They want to learn firsthand. They'd rather learn things the hard way. Allow them to make mistakes in areas that won't harm them too much. Give them choices and discuss with them the natural consequences of their choices."

For many young teens, middle school will be the first time to switch classrooms and teachers every hour. They are not the oldest at the school anymore; now they are the youngest. Many will have their first job, no matter how small. Perhaps they will first experience holding hands, kissing, or giving the appearance of actually liking a friend of the opposite sex. The first real dance usually occurs during middle school and, most likely, the first real crush. For the first time, peers become critically important, and friendships are expected to last forever. Peers become a major support system.

On the down side, these firsts may include a first experience with drugs, as the national average age for the onset of substance use is 12.8 years. Clear, understanding communication becomes even more important as a preventive measure. When middle schoolers feel understood and free to talk about what bothers them, they feel less stressed and have less need to seek relief outside of the family.

With their new ability to think abstractly comes the ability for young teens to look at the future. The intensity of feelings, however, floods in and distorts the view.[4] Having never felt this intense before, this "in love," this "heartbroken," this "accepted and understood," this "misunderstood," they often assume neither they nor anyone else will ever feel this same feeling in this same way. The present orientation that young adolescents typically feel, coupled with their concept of invincibility, can become a problem if mature parents are not still closely, but respectfully, involved in their lives. For example, a heartbroken young teen is less likely to get depressed when a parent understands and listens.

Young teenagers at this early stage desperately need love and nurturance, and if they do not feel it at home from their family, they will look for it elsewhere. Experiencing love and support that encourages and empowers them, not suffocates them, will give them the emotional fuel needed to navigate the currents of adolescence to achieve a fifth developmental task of the teen years, that of developing a unique and solid sense of *identity*.

"Adjusting," was the answer of children of friends when I asked them what the biggest problems are in middle school. Webster defines *adjust* as "to settle, to resolve . . . to adapt, to conform oneself to new conditions, . . . to achieve mental and behavioral balance between one's own needs and the demands of others." My young advisers clarified their answer this way: "Adjusting—to new friends, teachers, counselors, getting used to the new schedule, being on campus and not getting lost."

The demands on middle schoolers are everywhere: from teachers, principal, parents, security guards, coaches, and even older kids. Ruth says that the biggest surprise for her was experiencing "how mean the eighth graders were. They call you names and stand in your way, yelling, 'I'm not moving, so you have to move.'" Her older brother says that the biggest surprise was "the number of people there," and he adds, "You felt lost in the crowd."

"The hardest thing is conflict management," explains Linda Kewin, a former vice-principal at Arrowview Middle School in California:

> Kids don't know how to deal with large numbers of other kids. They suddenly move from that self-contained classroom where they've got one person they really latch onto and thirty other predictable classmates, into a situation where they now have many adults and hundreds of kids.

Judy Kissinger, former vice-principal of San Bernardino and Cajon High Schools, adds, "They feel so insignificant, invisible, and insecure."

YOUR MIDDLE SCHOOLER'S COCOON: UNDERSTANDING AND FIRM SUPPORT

Like a caterpillar transforming into a butterfly, your young teen probably is having some crazy thoughts. Imagine a caterpillar's thoughts when his body begins to secrete a thread that he wraps around him: "What's happening to me? I can't move very much. My head! What's that coming out of my head? I feel so tired, so lethargic. I can't see. The hairs on my body are falling off!" Similarly, in this vulnerable stage of your child's life, she feels unbalanced; she's going through dramatic size and shape changes, feeling at times confused and disoriented, being messy and disengaged, and questioning previously held values. As she goes through this time of untangling and unloosening, she needs a firm cocoon/structure to protect her—not too rigid and not too soft.

Taking the caterpillar comparison a bit further—once it has metamorphosed into a butterfly, the creature begins to exercise its newly formed wings as it pushes against the walls of the chrysalis to break it open. That is how it gains the strength necessary to fly. So it is with the young teen who needs the proper level of firmness from his parents—a structure hard enough to contain his reactions and yet not so rigid as to prevent his ever emerging to fly. Here are some examples of parental responses to a young teen exercising wings:

- Too Soft: "Well, if all of the kids are going to do it, I guess you can stay out until 11:00 P.M., too."

- Appropriately Firm: "I understand you really, really want to play basketball until 11:00 P.M. Thursday. You need to be in bed by 9:30 since it's a school night, so I'll pick you up at 9:00."

- Too rigid: "I can't believe you even asked such a stupid thing. You're so irresponsible. Just for that, you're staying home all day! And don't ask me about Friday either."

If a gentle person seeing a struggling butterfly decides to help it by cracking open the chrysalis, he has in fact doomed it to die, as its wings will not have enough strength to fly.

Similarly, parents who become rescuers when they see their young teen struggling, actually doom their child never to really fly. Rescuing can take the form of being overprotective or intervening to prevent natural consequences from occurring or becoming too involved in his daily life (having him sit with you rather than his team at his soccer game).

During this time in their lives, your children need instead to develop an attachment to the school and to new friends, which Judy Kissinger adds, comes as "they become involved in school activities, right away—yearbook, athletics, clubs." Resnick et al. discovered that middle school kids who found a genuine connection with school had less emotional distress and fewer thoughts of suicide.[5] This school connection meant they felt cared for by teachers and they felt that their teachers had high expectations for them.

REMEMBER THAT MIDDLE SCHOOL KIDS ARE PEOPLE

Adolescents need their parents to understand where they are coming from. They are entering a new season of life in which their needs seem contradictory at times—they need a sense of power; they need a release of the tremendous tension they can feel at times; and they need attention, stimulation, self-expression, rebellion, and affiliation. In *I Know Why the Caged Bird Sings,* Maya Angelou writes, "The intensity with which young people live demands that they blank out as often as possible."[6]

As you learn to understand your young teen developmentally, remember that her life task during this period of time is to begin to develop a solid identity. That means she must think through who she is, what she believes, what is important to her, and how she can make a contribution, so that she can claim these values as her own.

Your teen needs you not only to understand his life and world, but also to believe in him. To make this point, family researcher Beavers tells a story about an Arkansas boy who taught chickens to dance.[7] When people asked the boy how he could accomplish these tasks with chickens, the boy explained these steps:

> First off, you must believe the chicken isn't evil, isn't making every attempt to thwart your hopes and dreams. It's hard to train a chicken if you think it has it in for you.

> Second, you reward the chicken with something the chicken likes, not with what you think he ought to like or with whatever's handy.

> Third, you reward approximations of the behavior desired. If you wait until the chicken spins all the way around before rewarding, you will have to wait a long time between opportunities to be effective. A turn of the head to the left, a foot moving in that direction will merit a quick reward.

> Fourth, you ignore behavior that is not what you want—we would call it undancing behavior. The combination of alert rewards and careful neglect of the unwanted is a powerful tool in producing a dancing chicken.

Fifth, punishment is not necessary in creating dancing chickens, but it can discourage some other behaviors and therefore might have some usefulness. However, punishment only works when there have been frequent, consistent rewards. Without that, the punishment becomes the reward of attention and encourages exactly what it is supposed to eliminate. As Beavers writes, "A starved chicken just doesn't dance or do much of anything else very well."

Although this story is a little too behaviorist for my personal taste, it has merit. Note the first point, that you must believe or assume that the chicken is not evil or out to get you. It is not trying to thwart all of your efforts to achieve your hopes and goals. The rest of the steps will not make any difference without the first one! Chickens and young teens work the same way in this regard. What you assume about them influences how they respond to you. Sarah knows her mother thinks she does drugs; so maybe she should just prove her right. Roger has heard his father call him stupid and dumb for years; now he has begun to believe it himself. One of Michelangelo's toughest battles in life was with his father (whom he clearly loved), who assumed when Michelangelo was a young teenager that he could never make any real money or accomplish anything significant if he went into art.

Following this line of thinking, Principal Otis, speaking as a father, said,

> We quickly catch them doing things wrong, and we spend most of our time in our communication talking about a very small part of their lives . . . we need to correspondingly catch them doing things right and reward them and acknowledge them, hug them, send little notes to them. My wife and I used to send little notes to them at school, just to say they're important.

Lance and Ginny worked at their communication with their kids. Since asking the usual question, "How was school today?" elicited the usual answer, "Fine," they learned to create a conversation to get the insight they were looking for. They rephrased the question, saying, "Tell me about school." They suggest that parents of quieter kids say: "Tell me. Think about, write about, demonstrate, sing a song, create a rap, but tell me about school. I don't care how you do it. Write me a poem, dance it out, act it out." When you say, "Tell me about . . ." to your young teen, you are more likely to get more than a one-word response. It is an open-ended request that invites communication.

BELIEVE IN YOUR KIDS

Jim Kissinger, principal of Golden Valley Middle School in southern California, states, "You have to keep looking at what this kid can be . . . they're our future. . . . They've been given a lot of raw deals; they're not just what you see today. You can't be judgmental." He added, "They may be sullen one day and friendly and outgoing the next. They're really just like big third-graders." A visitor to his school campus of 1,126 students can see that his philosophy works; from the self-contained alternative classroom with learning handicapped kids to the gifted and talented classrooms, his teachers work with him to provide successes for the students. In his words, "Success breeds self-esteem."

PRACTICE TIPS FOR SURVIVAL AND SUCCESS

1. Listen to the *words* your teen uses. The words will give you clues as to what is important to him. When it is appropriate and the words are not middle school slang, use them occasionally when you talk together.

   Have him define words and terms for you. He will think you are an antique, but you will understand him better.

2. Listen to the words and phrases you use when talking to your teen. Negative phrases are counterproductive. Instead of "Don't you dare go out until your room is picked up," try "Please pick up your clothes before you go out." Workplace psychologist Dr. J. Mitchell Perry writes that even adult workers are more cooperative when a manager uses positive language. "Optimism is

learnable. It's the single most powerful and easiest way to change your behavior."[8] Try this with your middle schooler. Instead of answering "Not too bad," answer "That's pretty good." Instead of "Don't give me any of your lame excuses," try "Tell me what you plan to do about it."

3. Study your teen as an anthropologist might study a native of another culture. Pay attention to what he spends his money on. Money is always a good clue to what is important.

4. Try this fun communication exercise with your family to help everyone see how easily communication gets distorted. First, draw a simple design of squares and circles. The design might look something like this:

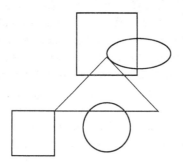

Keep the designs hidden until you are ready to start. Pair up, preferably parent-child, but any combination of two will work. Have each pair sit in chairs with backs together, so the partners will not be able to see each other's work. Give one person a design and her partner a pencil and a blank piece of paper on a clipboard. Have the person with the design communicate verbally to her partner how to draw the same design. When finished, compare the originals with the duplicates. Then switch tasks and designs and repeat. Discuss the results, and what those results might teach about communication.

5. To help you and your family understand and respect how parents and teens think differently, discuss together the following:

Michael Jordan ended his basketball career and began a career in baseball. (Of course, he later switched back to basketball.) To make the switch, he had to change his way of thinking, his view of teamwork, and his skill development. What specific changes did he have to make? For example, baseball requires developing individual skills such as hitting, pitching, throwing, running, sliding. Basketball requires individual skills, but also a higher level of unselfish play in which one player may be regularly called upon to give up opportunities to score so that the team has a greater chance of winning. Giving assists is as important as being a good shooter.

Brainstorm to see what other changes you come up with. Discuss the different mindsets (worldviews) needed for each sport to be played well. Discuss together the ways that thinking about sports skills and sports teamwork can be compared to thinking about family teamwork and communication. Parenting during the middle school years requires a different focus and different team dynamics than during the early childhood years. Young teens need to give more input into family matters and parents need to listen with respect.

6. Learn to reflect feelings and meanings. When your daughter complains that her friends went skating without her, you can say, "You must feel really left out." When your son threatens to tattoo his arm, you can say, "You really want to be different from us, to show the world you have your own mind." Then you can talk together if a different solution is needed. To your son you might add, "What's another way to show you're different from us?" Seeing yourself as a mirror to your teen helps keep you from being judgmental and critical.

7. Join a group for parents of young teens. You may be amazed at the similarities of some of the experiences. Often just knowing that other middle schoolers are doing the same things as yours helps you deal with this growth stage more effectively.

8. Volunteer at the middle school in a position where your child

and her friends will not even know you are there—she likely will not want to see you there, but you can learn a great deal about middle school kids by doing this.

9. Volunteer to drive to school events and take other kids. I learned a lot about my kids just by driving to basketball games, volleyball games, and science field trips.

2
SECRET #2:
WALK CAREFULLY
BALANCE SUPPORT AND CONTROL

J ocelyn skipped school today. She is a good kid, gets *A*s in her honors classes, is a mature thirteen, is very involved in community activities and girls' soccer, and has a lead part in a community playhouse production. This is not the first time she has failed to show up for school. She missed two days last week. She is a clever girl, though. Her parents never got the automatic computer phone call from school informing them of her absence because she recently had the school office change her records to show her friend's personal telephone number as her own.

"Leave me alone," she says. "I can take care of myself. You raised me to be independent. Let me make my own decisions." Jocelyn tells her soccer coach she is "so stressed out" but does not say why. She has been lying to her family, stealing small items from them at first, and then an expensive watch. Her mother has noticed that some of Jocelyn's own expensive possessions are no longer around, her grades are tumbling, and her friends are changing.

Jocelyn's mother and father are at odds. Her father, Robert, wants to believe what Jocelyn says. He has been lenient with her, trusting that she has indeed bought his earnest lectures on trust and honesty. Her mother, having come from her own high school years of truancy and promiscuity, feels Jocelyn needs strong rules and strict guidelines. She cannot understand her husband's softness and has determined to protect her daughter from the very things she did, no matter what it costs. Jocelyn's younger brother knows more than he tells. He loves his older sister, but she frightens him with her crazy behavior. He feels caught between loyalty to his sister and respect for his parents. The signs of trouble have been there, but Jocelyn's family did not want to see them before. Now it is almost too late. Is she pregnant? On drugs? Drinking? In trouble with the law? What can they do?

While it is almost never too late for helping a young teenager, families frequently find themselves precariously close to being too late. Changing how you balance support and control now with your young teenager could stem the tide of unreleased resentments later. Encouraging openness and honesty early on may help avert the deadly progression of the kind of bitterness that Jocelyn played out in her behaviors.

CHECKING WHAT YOU MODEL

Under stress, we use the coping skills we have seen modeled. Issler and Habermas, in their book on learning, use an illustration of a child performing the Heimlich maneuver, a skill he had learned through the modeling of others.[1] This example has great meaning for our family because of an experience Kristopher had in eighth grade. In his science classroom one day, he saw one of his class-mates choking at the sink, with bubbles of saliva forming around his mouth. In this tense situation, Kristopher ran back and per-formed the Heimlich maneuver until the boy coughed up a piece of food. Kristopher had never done this before. The only way he knew anything about it was because he listened and watched when his father demonstrated it one night.

In normal daily living, we all do what we have seen modeled. In her national column, Linda Ellerbee discussed her years of smoking and how she finally quit two years ago. She realized that she could still get lung cancer years down the road. "Worse yet," she la-mented, "no matter how fine I might feel about the choice I've made, nothing can make up for this: Both my grown children smoke. Wonder where they learned that?"[2]

Our children learn from what we model in our own behavior, whether we want them to or not. Especially if we do not have the necessary openness in the family to discuss it, they will automatically pick up our negative behaviors and act them out in other situations without thinking. Sergeant Charlie Wilhite, a drug recognition expert with the Sheriff's Department of the County of Riverside, tells of one young teen he caught smoking marijuana. When the sergeant took away his marijuana pipe, the boy was in tears. Wilhite explains, "What I found out was that he was quite upset because this was his father's favorite marijuana pipe and he was going to get in deep trouble when he got home. Much of this is learned behavior. These kids emulate their parents."

At the Loma Linda University Learning Center, Dr. Robert Boehm explains that when students see teachers doing something secretly that is different from what is taught, they are said to be receiving the tacit curriculum, the one that is never talked about. In families, when middle schoolers see their parents modeling the opposite of what is expected of the children, they, too, are under a tacit curriculum, one that is much more powerful than what their parents say.

FALSE IMAGES

Your perception of your young teen may not always be acccurate. We often misjudge them and base our perceptions on what we remember being like as a young teen. Sometimes even what we are thinking at the moment will color how we see them. I had a lesson in perception one day when I was out jogging through a field near our home. As I glanced ahead, I thought I saw a gazelle perched very still on a little mound, scouting the area for danger. Finally, closer and with the help of the sun, I saw the gazelle silhouette for what it was—an old, weathered tree stump. Knowing full well that gazelles do not live on the free range in Southern California, I had to ask myself why I had even entertained the idea. I had seen gazelles on mounds before, but they were thousands of miles away in Africa. On my jog in California this particular day I had been thinking about that trip. Images of zebras, gazelles, and elephants circulated in my mind. So, when I saw a hazy, ambiguous shape off in the distance, I projected meaning onto it, based on what I was thinking.

To understand projection, think of a slide projector. You think you are seeing an actual image, but you are only seeing what the projector reflects. Even preteens can understand how this works. Several years ago, when Michèle was ten, she came home from school complaining that her friend Grace had called her several names, taunting her. Attempting to console her, I asked if that had hurt her feelings. She replied, "No, I just told her that she was projecting on me."

Parents often fall into the same trap of projection. Hank was a father who had lived an unfettered life during his high school years, acting out frequently on his sexual urges. He had met his wife, Carol, when a mutual friend jokingly told him that she was a hot date. It was no surprise, then, to hear him talk about the boys his daughter was hanging out with. He was convinced that all they thought about was sex and that she would never be safe with any of them. For this reason, he clamped down on her activities, forbidding any mixed gender skating parties or dances. Hank was projecting onto these boys something he had never shared with his family. His parents had rarely been home and his emotional needs as a boy were left unmet. He had never learned how to have a friend who also happened to be a girl, so he fantasized and related to girls solely as sexual beings. In contrast, his daughter had wisely chosen her friends; the boys she knew had both the interest and the capability to be just good friends. Hank's projection, however, made for some stormy arguments and hurt feelings on both sides before the issue was resolved.

Hank's psychological myopia led him to underestimate his daughter's character and skills.[3] Psychological myopia is a type of projection, or *dis-ease*, of the parent's psyche that affects vision. Equal danger can come when you overestimate your child's skills. Psychological myopia of either type can keep you from really getting to know and understand your young teenager.

Stereotyping is another kind of projection and misperception.

Healthy families experience very little stereotyping of family members—Mom is not labeled as the softie and Dad the enforcer. Sometimes Mom is soft and sometimes she is the firmer one. One child is not categorized as the achiever and another as the beauty queen. Since members are not pigeon-holed, they are free to learn and grow and have many traits that may change over time.

CHECKING YOUR BELIEFS ABOUT HEALTHY FAMILIES

Healthy families with young teens have some beliefs in common. Check your own attitudes against the following list:

1. *Belonging is important.*
   Every young teen carries a deep need to belong. My grandmother once described some people to me when I was a teenager saying, "They're nice people, like us." I smiled at her comparison but warmed to her "us" concept. We were "us." We were a family with four kids, two parents, five grandparents, and aunts, uncles, cousins. The us was bigger than a collection of you and me. The us was a holding web, a network of support. I would always be uniquely me, and I would always be part of this family. Even today that is part of who I am.

2. *Behavior can have many causes.*
   Examples of this are everywhere. Susie's father spends less time with her now that she is twelve and boy-crazy. Susie has not just become this way because her hormones have gone wild. Another motivator is her need for more attention from her father. Since she does not get that, she tries to get attention from other males. In addition, she feels great pressure from her grandfather about grades. Their family tradition has been for the oldest child in the family to attend Harvard. Already in middle school, Susie is letting him down. Depressed about disappointing him, she has given up on her homework, deciding that it just does not matter what she does. Susie needs support from her father and her family.

Cassandra sneaked vodka and drank until she passed out at a family gathering. This did not just occur because she was trying to feel accepted by the older cousins. In fact, the stress and depression inside of her had built over several years. Her step-father loves her, but not in the same way that he cherishes his biological daughter. Her own biological father lavishes his affections on his other daughter and ignores Cassie. Not wanting to seem ungrateful, she has hidden her feelings of jealousy and of not belonging. Family gatherings always have brought up painful reminders she wants to block out. Drinking at age thirteen was her attempt to keep things hidden and protect the family from having to deal with her hurt. Cassie needs support.

3. *Mistakes can be learning experiences.*
No one can be perfect, and no one is completely helpless. In Jared's family, apologies come easily because no one is expected to be perfect. A spilled coke is just a spilled coke. Accidents do not mean someone is clumsy or bad, and a mistake is never a reason for criticism.

Ellen's family believes in the value of mistakes. When Ellen's bad attitude led to her ejection from the soccer game, she felt sad, embarrassed, and angry. She knew, however, that her dad would not punish her further. He would let her learn from the consequences of her actions. That was the last time Ellen displayed that same behavior. Her dad knew how to support her while allowing her to face consequences.

Heidi's family understands that losing, like mistakes, can bring lessons. The family is comfortable talking about losing, and people are seen as fallible human beings. When Heidi tried out for a new sport and did not make the team, no one saw her as a failure. Heidi then decided to put her efforts into learning German and played basketball just for fun.

4. *Families carry patterns through the generations.*
A family who understands this realizes that sometimes unresolved issues are sitting on top of a stack of conflicting family

messages. Mandy was angry that her parents would not let her ride her bike to school but regularly let her brother walk to the neighborhood park. Her family was willing to stop and evaluate with these kinds of questions: What is the end goal we all want? What are our family messages about girls and safety? About boys and safety? What do you think about the differences? In this way, Mandy's family was able to talk about unhealthy family patterns. They discovered they had overprotected the girls for generations. From her great-grandfather on down, boys had been treated as more capable than girls. Together, Mandy's family decided to make some changes.[4]

WORKING AT THE BALANCE OF SUPPORT AND CONTROL

Several years ago a large study was conducted on families with teenagers over a period of several years.[5] The results produced a schema for categorizing families and predicting teenage delinquency. Each family fit into one of four types, using two axes: support and control (limits). Each category was titled and observations were made. One type of family had a much larger number of teenagers in trouble. One type had very few.

Quadrant I was titled *Authoritarian* and was characterized by high control and low support. Parents in these families made statements like "I don't care what you think. No football games for you! Don't ask again and wipe that smirk off your face." Quadrant II was titled *Authoritative.* It was characterized by both high support and high control. Parent statements in these families might be "You really want to go to the game tonight. I'd like you to have your homework finished first." Quadrant III was labeled *Uninvolved* and showed both low support and low control. These parents had limited interaction with their children. They might not know or care about the football game. Quadrant IV was labeled *Permissive* and was characterized by high support and low control. Their parent statements might include "Come home from the game when you're ready."

I AUTHORITARIAN High Control Low Support	II AUTHORITATIVE High Control High Support
III UNINVOLVED Low Control Low Support	IV PERMISSIVE Low Control High Support

Authoritarian families (I) produced the largest number of teens in trouble. Authoritative families (II) had the lowest number. Surprisingly, uninvolved families (III) had fewer teens in trouble than did the authoritarian families. A high degree of control, when not balanced with an equally high degree of support, can develop into rigid legalism which the teenager reacts against in order to meet his growing need for autonomy. Young teens with authoritarian parents often feel like prisoners with life sentences. Pediatrician Ed Elmendorf adds that they may feel this for the duration of their life. These prison *lifers* will take big risks to escape their sentence; they know they will have more consequences to face if they are caught, but without hope of reprieve, they do not care. "Whatever," they say.

PARENTAL CONTROL

In order to work on the control part of this parental balance, we all need a clear understanding of the three main types of control and their levels of effectiveness.[6] Think about where you fit in the following descriptions:

1. Coercion
   Recent studies show that parents who use coercion rarely have teens who conform to their expectations. *Coercion* can be defined as "restraining or dominating by force" or "the use of direct and arbitrary force." (A sample test item used in the research for coercion was, "This parent punished me by not letting me do

things I really enjoy.") We may think that because we can force our middle schoolers to do what we want, our expectations have been met. In reality, however, the opposite has occurred. Forced against their will, they commit to do the opposite. While parents may achieve short-term compliance by administering severe consequences, the middle school child parented in this way rarely internalizes a sense of cooperativeness and conformity with his parents' expectations. The more harsh the coercion, the more resistant the teenager becomes. Hence, when a parent continues to use coercion as his primary parenting mode, he is, in fact, inviting his child to become reactive and rebellious.

2. Love Withdrawal

   Love withdrawal, threatened or actual withdrawal of affection, is the opposite of unconditional love. (A sample test item: "This parent will not talk to me when I displease him/her.") This type of parental control is played out when a seventh grader calls her mother from a friend's house, says one wrong word, and her mother slams down the phone. The use of love withdrawal as a parenting technique teaches the young teen that she is loved only when she performs up to her parents' expectations. Since no one can perform up to another's expectations all of the time, she is in constant danger of losing her parents' love. The ever-present pressure to perform becomes too much, and she will sabotage herself in an effort to get relief from the pressure. Parental control based on love withdrawal was found to increase problem behaviors, including substance abuse.

3. Guidance

   A third type of parental control, *induction*, is defined as "placing rational maturity demands on children to make them aware of the consequences of their actions." Induction means guidance more than control—giving logical, reasonable consequences that are related to the problem, not as a punitive effort, but as a learning tool. (Sample test item: "This parent explains to me how good I should feel when I do right.") In the studies, parental induction proved to help the young teens move more gracefully through the developmental changes of adolescence and had a significantly reduced number and risk of problem behaviors.

As you evaluate your own style of control, avoid the pitfall of those parents who are convinced that it is in their job description to always tell their young teens what to do, how to do it, and when to do it, but all under the guise of *just helping*. This is not just helping. It is controlling, and it is counterproductive to your young teen's development of a strong, responsible inner self. In cases where parents add harshness to the high control, boys in particular suffer low self-esteem and lower grades. Parents need to remember that it is natural for the young teen to irrevocably change the family. The job of the parents is to listen, respect, guide, and begin to release. Working together to make change, the whole family benefits.

PARENTAL SUPPORT

Even a plant needs more than a strong stake to determine its growth direction. It needs fertilizer, water, good soil, and sunlight. In the same way, middle schoolers need parental support, defined as giving warmth, acceptance, personal value, and nurturance.[7] The more that parents used praise, encouragement, attention, approval, and affection, the more their young teens felt open to communicate with their parents and chose not to use drugs. These same young teens, parented in a supportive way, were more popular and had higher grades, higher self-esteem, and fewer psychological and behavioral problems. Young teen girls, who tend to suffer a big drop in self-esteem during these years, especially need a warm, supportive relationship with parents as a buffer against that drop.

RESPECT + SUPPORT + LIMITS + EMPATHY = PATHWAY TO HEALTHY TEENS

Ginott defines empathy as the ability to respond genuinely to our child's moods and feelings without being infected by them.[8] So how can a parent stay empathic while concentrating on all those other issues? Added to that, even though your intentions may be good, the end result may not even be close to what you wanted. Support may sound different to your middle school child than it does to you.

Here is a typical scenario for a thirteen-year-old girl, complaining in front of her bathroom mirror seconds before she needs to leave the house for school:

> Daughter: *moan, moan . . .* "I just can't go to school. My hair looks awful! I can't be seen like this."

> Good-intentioned Mom: "But, honey, I think you look really cute that way. Just a little more hair spray and . . ."

Now let's look at the daughter's silent split-second analysis and interpretation of what her mother just said:

> "But": *So I'm wrong and you're right. I disagree with you.*

> "honey": *Too sweet. I'm too mad to want to hear sweetness.*

> "cute": *I don't want to look cute.*

> "that way": *See, it is different and weird.*

> "Just use . . .": *And now you're telling me what to do.*

> Daughter's conclusion (said loudly and with stomping): "You *never* understand! I can't go like this!!"

And now for the informed parent's response:

> Mom (shrugging shoulders nonchalantly): "I know what you mean, I just hate it when my hair won't cooperate."

> Daughter's interpretation: *Oh wow, Mom understands.*

> Daughter's verbal response: "Well, guess I'd better get ready and go."

The key is to respect and listen to your young teen's thoughts, ideas, and feelings without rebuttal or belittling. However she feels at that particular moment is how it is for her (even if it may seem exaggerated or unrealistic to you). Reflect back to her what you sense she is feeling. Once she feels understood, she has no need to be reactive and she is able to figure out what to do next. Two separate studies found that when supportive families allowed teens to openly express their views, the teens matured more rapidly. If a young teen senses that his perspective is valued enough to be listened to, he is more likely to drop his defensive wall and gain the freedom to look more objectively at his own views and yours.

LEARNING HOW TO LISTEN

Webster defines the expression *in one ear and out the other* as "through one's mind without making an impression." Parents complain daily that what they say to their teens goes in one ear and out the other. In fact, parents do the same thing to what their teens say, giving it little importance. The opposite of this would be to learn how to listen in such a way as to allow what is heard to make an impression, and even to increase the range of what is heard. James gave a great principle in the New Testament: "Everyone should be quick to listen, slow to speak and slow to become angry" (James 1:19b).

All of us can develop this listening skill. A few years ago, as our family strolled through a noisy street in Chinatown, Los Angeles, Kristopher stopped and asked, "Listen, do you hear that?" In the midst of firecrackers and bustling movements, he said, "They're playing mah jong. Up there, in that building, up a couple of floors, I think. Listen, you can hear them slap the tiles. Now they're mixing the tiles."

None of the rest of us could hear a thing—at least until we also had stopped and concentrated on the faint sounds emanating from the open window of the apartment building. As we tuned down the more dramatic outside noises, we could hear the distinct sounds of mah jong being played.

Why was Kristopher able to hear and quickly discern the meaning of those sounds while we were not even aware of them? The previous summer he was part of a team of five students who won a trip to Hong Kong in an academic competition. While there, Kristopher had seen small groups of people playing mah jong daily up and down the back streets of Hong Kong. He was familiar with the sounds, and he knew what they meant. This familiarity coupled with his natural sense of curiosity helped him develop ears to hear.

To be able to show support to your young teen, you also need ears to hear. At first it may seem impossible to listen for hidden needs or for hurt feelings underneath the noise and melodrama of her world. However, by becoming familiar with developmental changes and needs and finding out what is important to your teen, what she is sensitive to, and what she likes to do for fun, you will increase your ability to hear what is being said indirectly. Gottman, in his research on parenting emotionally intelligent children, stresses the importance of knowing the specifics of your child's world in order to increase your connection with him.[9] Gottman describes emotionally intelligent children as able to manage their own emotions, relate well to people, have good friendships, be resilient, and do better academically. It is as if they have an "IQ that is about people and the world of feelings."[10]

With ears to hear you can avoid being judgmental. Instead of responding, "Don't treat your friend that way. No wonder you never get asked to do anything, with an attitude like that," you are able to say, having heard what is being said without words, "You must have felt hurt when Sam didn't invite you to his party. Can we talk about it?" Sometimes young teens do not know why they are so angry. Getting the right word to describe what they are feeling can give them a new way to cope with it.

Suppose you skip the real listening and say, "Don't complain about how badly you played soccer today unless you're willing to practice, practice, practice. You'll never get anywhere until you decide to do some work." You are likely to hear in response, "Whatever." Instead, try, "So you had a bad day on the soccer field. That must be pretty frustrating for you." Your young teen will feel supported and understood; with no reason to react defensively, he will be likely to take responsibility. He may say, "Yeah, I think I'll ask the coach what I can do to get better."

Obviously, there is no quick-fix method. However, hearing and respecting your teen in this way brings change from the inside out, a maturing process. The resulting changes in behavior may be slower in coming, but they are longer lasting since they are coming from a growing sense of self. In contrast, quick superficial changes forced by a punitive parental response are rooted in compliance, not a sense of self. Compliance carries with it the strong possibility of a later negative payoff—resentment and bitterness or a spineless jellyfish approach to life (which often later results in depression). Support through listening is worth the effort.

SEEKING EFFECTIVE CONSEQUENCES

If you, like many parents, struggle to discover consequences that work, remember that effective consequences build responsibility, not resentment. Consequences can be positive or negative; they provide direction and help your middle schooler learn. If a response is too harsh or too lenient for the crime, you will not get the desired result from your young teen. Your middle schooler can contribute to your list of usable consequences. See the Tips section at the end of this chapter for some examples.

Since firm consequences may be needed at any time, make sure to set the stage for effectiveness by creating a generally positive atmosphere to balance those consequences. For example, occasionally take the kids a big bowl of popcorn or a cold drink on a hot day when you pick them up from school. Pay close attention to your teen's responses to you. Accept her feelings without judgment. That alone shows support and reduces her need to react. If she's getting more reactive or rebellious, your communication and relationship with her may be too heavy-handed (authoritarian). Increase your supportive behaviors and language and see what happens.

Use praise effectively. If you repeatedly say, "You're such a wonderful (or beautiful or talented) kid," it will lose its effectiveness and may even induce some contrary behavior. He's likely to think, "Oh, sure—but you don't really know everything I do" or "I wonder what you'll say when I really let you down." Instead, praise specific parts of something your teen does so he can draw his own conclusion, something like, "I guess I am pretty good." As a parent you can say, "I really enjoyed reading your paper on steroids. I learned some things I didn't know, and the way you organized your paragraphs made it easy for me to follow your thoughts."

KEEP WORKING ON BALANCE

Support and control need to be in balance. The mixture of elements in that balance changes as your young teen grows up, provided that she has learned what she needs to learn at a particular stage and that you have also. Parents need to set firm limits for their young teens, but they must also build in a way to introduce flexibility, increased choice, and privacy. Young teens should be allowed to choose the sports they play, the musical instruments they play, their friends, and their clothes (within limits).

A musician friend of ours, Glen Aubrey, was telling us recently how he was guiding his twelve-year-old daughter as she played music from *The Phantom of the Opera* on the piano. He described how her left hand methodically pounded out the deeper ominous tones as her right hand lightly played out the melody. He helped her to hear what happened each time she struck a key with her right hand—the music began immediately to die away, overpowered by the booming notes of the left hand. His suggestion was that she lighten the touch of the left hand so the melody could be heard. In a way, communicating with your young teen is similar to playing the piano. Even if much of your communication is lighter and nurturing, the part that is angry, rigid, loud, and intensely emphatic will overpower the kinder melody of your relationship, leaving a lingering sound of resentment. Happily for parents, we can continually work on finding the best balance in our interactions with our children.

PRACTICE TIPS FOR SURVIVAL AND SUCCESS
Do all you can to give your family positive experiences that tell your young teen in particular that you value his company, his ideas,

his interests, his unique contribution to the family.

1. Plan mini-vacations together. We always planned a one-day event to celebrate the "end of a fabulous summer." Some of our favorite choices were Disneyland, San Diego Wild Animal Park, San Diego Zoo, and Sea World. One year when airlines had a cheap promotional fare, we really went wild and flew to San Francisco for the day to visit Alcatraz and to eat great sourdough bread. Mini-vacations can come in a wide range of prices; look in the calendar section of your Sunday newspaper for museums, theme parks, music events, movies, outdoor theater, air shows—anything that strikes your family's fancy.

2. Make a list together as a family titled, "Twenty Things Our Family Should Do in Our Lifetime." Short-term events build family memories. Longer projects give the family focus and goals. Here are some examples:

   - Have a long evening picnic at the beach or in the mountains or in the countryside. (Take two sets of car keys in case one set is lost in the sand!)

   - Become good friends with a family from a different racial background.

   - Visit the country your ancestors came from.

   - Help a single-parent family once a month for a year.

   - Ride horses in the country together.

   - Create a family scrapbook that tells the story of your family. Include pictures, mementos, and drawings made by the children. Use one of the paper scissors that cuts with a decorative edge. Add to the design extra bits of colored paper, stickers, and appropriate phrases cut from magazines. Work on it together.

■ Make Christmas ornaments together, such as the old-fashioned ones made from dough.

■ Write poems together. Give each person a piece of paper, a pencil, and ten minutes to write a poem. Good titles to use: Greed, Money, Friends, Honesty, Teams. Read the poems to the family.

3. In the following chart are some suggested consequences for broken rules, part of the control half of the balance we are discussing. Asking your child to help you come up with effective consequences for goof-ups is a way to expand your understanding and at the same time show that you value her thoughts. Remember that a consequence is for learning and for changing behavior.

Crimes	Consequences
Home fifteen minutes past curfew	Subtract fifteen minutes from curfew the next time
Stealing	Community service work
Bad language	Dollar fine in family jar

If your child is caught stealing, first sit down and talk. This behavior may be your teen's reaction to feeling he has been given unfair treatment. Then you might designate community service work, such as with the Salvation Army, so that your teen can help feed the poor or needy.

A consequence for using bad language could be to put one dollar in a glass jar marked "$ for Wise Words." The dollar is a fine that will help all family members remember to use wiser language. The family can decide together how they will use the money accumulated. It might be used to buy a book for the family or to give to a cause.

3
SECRET #3:
ALWAYS KNOCK FIRST
MAINTAIN FIRM, FLEXIBLE
BOUNDARIES

S ome people have computers in their cars that tell them where they are. Since we don't have such global positioning systems for families, we need maps and compasses to help orient ourselves. Paths lead us to destinations. Boundaries protect us as we go along. Dr. Mary Pipher writes, "When we erase lines, kids have no protection and adults have no dignity or obligations."[1] A boundary is similar to an invisible line that separates one person from another. Kate, a physician friend, says that she pictures her personal boundary as her "emotional skin." That helps her remember its purpose: to define who she is and to protect her. Physiologically, she knows that her skin wraps around her body shape, and that she alone is responsible for the care of all of the organs and tissues within. She knows that her mind is within her boundary. She also knows that her physical skin protects her from the harmful bacteria outside her body. She knows that if she touches someone else, the nerve endings just under her skin will tell her which part belongs to her and which part belongs to the other person.

PERSONAL BOUNDARIES

Henry Cloud in his book, *When Your World Makes No Sense,* compares personal boundaries to property lines that delineate where responsibility lies.[2] Your neighbor Sam does not need to come over weekly to trim your hedges, and his wife Shari might be highly offended if you barged into their home with cleaning supplies and started scrubbing their kitchen stove. Your property lines define the limits of responsibility for both of you. On a personal level, within your own boundaries lie your thoughts, feelings, use of time and money, choices, limits, behaviors, hopes, and dreams, for which you alone are responsible.

Years ago, I drove a car with a verbal computerized warning system. With the turn of the ignition key, a voice would speak to me from the car's innards, "All monitored systems functioning." The voice informed me if one system was not working. I could then make the necessary changes before leaving for the day. In the evening, the same voice might declare, "Your headlights are on," thus preserving the battery's life. If only we were this careful about monitoring ourselves, family communication would be less stressed. We would be guided by messages such as these: "You overstepped your limits." "Your anger is towards your boss, not your family." "Your emotional energy account has been depleted." Without an audible internal monitoring system, we need to pay careful attention to our personal emotional boundaries.

The healthiness of your boundaries could be measured by their firmness and flexibility. Sandi (age 13) says she always "feels her mother's feelings," and Tamara (age 12) says she and her mother often tell each other how they should feel, commenting, for example, "You shouldn't let that upset you." Their boundaries are too weak; they do not define and protect well enough. While such weak boundaries allow extra stress to seep in, rigid boundaries create a pressure-cooker atmosphere for stress. Jack's father isolates himself from the family. Sherry has decided never to tell anyone how she really feels. Their rigid boundaries will not allow for calm, clear communication.

Good personal boundaries allow each person to have her own

personal feelings regardless of what someone else is feeling. Jon's boundaries are permeable, yet firm; they allow him to hear and understand his son's plight without getting depressed. When his son Cam told him he was in trouble at school for skipping class and smoking, Jon listened and didn't feel like a failure. He asked Cam how he would like to remedy the situation. Together they decided Cam would volunteer some hours to help his teacher after school.

BOUNDARIES BETWEEN PARENTS

While you can never control the behavior of your spouse, the attitudes and actions with which you respond to his or her behavior will have some effect on the children. Even in families with an alcoholic parent, the actions of the nondrinking parent towards the drinking parent can greatly influence whether the children drink.[3] Researchers discovered that when a nondrinking parent supported drinking behaviors and organized family life around the alcoholic, more of the children in the family would develop drinking problems. The opposite effect occurred when the parent found the drinking behavior to be distasteful and did not allow it to interfere in family activities and rituals. (Rituals are routine activities such as eating dinner together around a table, celebrating birthdays, going to church.) Although one parent is modeling drinking, the other parent can model a very different attitude and influence others in the family that way.

In some families, the parents have differing and irreconcilable opinions relating to the treatment of their children. The next chapter on negotiation addresses this issue in more depth.

FIRMING UP BOUNDARIES BETWEEN PARENT AND MIDDLE SCHOOLER

Weak boundaries between a parent and a young teen create stress in their relationship. A mother who has poor boundaries with a young teen (almost as if the teen were an extension of herself) will often interpret the differences between her and her child as disloyalty—"How could she do this to me? She should agree with me. She should think as I do. She should be a leader as I was."

David says his sixth and eighth grade children laugh whenever he or his wife tries to set limits with them. Sue says that both her husband and her seventh grader refuse to take her seriously, and both treat her as the child in the family. Teresa's parents are having marital difficulties, and since Teresa's mother does not trust her husband, she has Teresa, thirteen, and her older sister follow him home from work. The parental boundaries in all of these families are so fuzzy and permeable that they prevent the family from communicating and functioning in a healthy way. The parents here have disregarded the fact that children of any age are not created with the capacity to carry the burden of parents' problems.

Research from the University of Tennessee found three things that happen when boundaries are weak and parents are intrusive in a child's development:[4]

1. Intrusiveness inhibits the child's development.

2. The child's anxiety increases.

3. The child does not develop the personal skills needed to cope with the stresses of dealing with people.

Too much intrusiveness can even invite aggressiveness. A middle schooler's room becomes a battleground for negotiating boundaries. When a frustrated father removed the bedroom door in an attempt to embarrass his son for his messiness, he got more than he bargained for. Anger over lack of privacy and his dad's intrusiveness produced volatile resistance, not cooperation.

Poor boundaries between mother and young teen have some correlation with suicidal feelings.[5] Many people who attempt suicide report multiple problems with their mothers. They do not think their mothers are capable of solving problems. Stress between the two usually leads to crises. They describe power struggles and disagreements over what is important. When feelings are communicated, the relationship becomes intense and highly charged, resulting in some kind of an outburst. One young teen, Christa, reported that when she tried to talk to her mother about her genuine feelings of depression, her mother would become highly anxious and tell her that she did not really feel that way, that someone else must have put that idea into her head. If Christa persisted in trying to be understood, her mother would become angry and yell at her. If they were talking on the telephone to each other, her mother would hang up on her.

The boundaries between a parent and young teen need to be more firm than they were when your teen was a young child. The need for privacy increases as puberty brings feelings of vulnerability. I remember watching our eighth-grade son and his friend, wearing the skimpy Speedo team swimsuits, dive into the pool for their first waterpolo game. With beach towels wrapped around them, they walked to the edge of the pool. In less than one second, the towels had dropped, and the two boys were in the water. I never did see them get out of the pool. They just appeared later, wrapped in large towels.

Parents need to respect this increased need for privacy by knocking on bedroom doors and waiting for an invitation to come in. One eighth grader's note to a friend summed it up:

> When something goes wrong in my life I go to my room. My room is about the only place I can go where I'll have privacy. A lot of times when I get hurt, I need a friend to lean on, a shoulder to cry on, but first I need to think. My room is a place where I can think and get my feelings sorted out. Music helps too, if I'm in a bad mood, I go to my room and listen to music, and I feel a lot better. Everyone needs to cry once in awhile and when I feel that need, I can go to my room and no one will know.

Laura described the subtle difference she feels when her parents show healthy boundaries and relate to her in a graceful way instead of with a parent's usual tendency to want control. When I asked her, "What has helped and what has hurt communication between you and your parents?" she responded:

Their showing interest in us, like wanting to know about us. I know I've really struggled a lot with this over the past year, feeling as though my parents cared too much and I don't get privacy, especially my Mom sometimes will always want to know "What's going on? Who called? What did he want?" And it made it hard for me to focus on her sometimes. And I don't get any privacy. It made me want to withdraw a little bit more. It made me really want to withdraw from her and not tell her or my dad some things. I find it so much better when parents show a lot of interest in you but not to the point where you feel like your life is being totally examined.

I asked her friend Ashley what it would sound like if parents were to relate to them in a less controlling way. She said,

More like wanting to know how I was, like, "How was school? How was your day?" and let me come to them and tell them problems I was having and then they can update on the problems I was having. Especially the phone thing, to not ask, "Who was that? What did she want?" And not be too focused. Give us our space. Be involved to a certain point and if we start to seem like we're withdrawing a little bit, then lay off a little bit and give us our space. That's important to me. Build up trust and point out to them when they're doing things right. Put trust in them in the beginning, give privileges, but if they don't live up to it, take privileges away.... Be a friend to your kid. Try to understand them.

Changing the boundaries between parents and young teens means moving away from being a control-oriented family to being a grace-filled family and letting God and natural consequences have the control with your kids. It means focusing your control tactics on the things you really can control, such as your attitudes, your own behaviors, your thoughts. It means making room in your family for grace. It means teaching and guiding your teens in ways that are meaningful to them. It means modeling the respect you expect from them. It means giving them choices and teaching them that choices have consequences. It means empowering them and not overprotecting them, allowing them to gain self-respect.

A good sense of humor helps us as parents remember our own boundaries. In contrast to most of our stereotypes of somber religious leaders, the Matthew Video Series from The Visual Bible International portrays a mirthful Jesus. One scene shows Jesus laughing with eyes twinkling as he picks up a four-foot-long plank of wood and holds it up to his eye, exclaiming:

> Why do you look at the speck of sawdust in your brother's eye and pay no attention to the plank in your own eye? How can you say to your brother, "Let me take the speck out of your eye," when all the time there is a plank in your own eye? (Matthew 7:3-4)[6]

Having a sense of humor does not minimize important lessons. Rather, it helps create a sense of openness to and acceptance of the message.

BUILDING HEALTHY FAMILY BOUNDARIES

For a family to be healthy, its boundaries need both to provide limits and to be permeable. Imagine a homeowner with a solid wall three feet thick and fifty feet high that totally surrounded his property, with no gates or windows. No one could enter or leave. With no interaction with people and resources outside, the residents inside would die. Now imagine a property bordered by a line so transparent that no one could tell which property belonged to whom. The residents would be confused and strangers would keep walking through your property. A healthy family needs a boundary that protects without cutting off access to the rest of the world.

The boundary around the entire family with a young teenager needs to be more permeable than it may have been three years before. Now the teen is making more demands for power and independence; he has more new friends and lots of new ideas, and he wants his parents to be open to them all. We found that having extra food and drinks around, putting up a basketball hoop or two, and offering to take kids to the beach were effective ways we could extend ourselves to our kids and their friends. We frequently had two to ten extra kids around the house during those years.

During the middle school years, we also tried to expose our kids to other cultures and many types of people, different from us by virtue of their age, ethnicity, or economic status. We were fortunate to travel together to Zaire, where my husband and I spoke at a conference and our kids helped with the babysitting for the conferees. In eighth grade, Kristopher traveled to New Zealand with a friend and his family for a three-week exchange program in which he interacted with many New Zealanders. That same year, he traveled with our church youth group to a Navajo reservation to teach Vacation Bible School for a week. Michèle was involved in volunteer work with people in convalescent homes and low income families. Our family had friends from varied backgrounds—one close friend lived in such a dangerous neighborhood that he asked us to pick him up at a restaurant, not at his home, for his safety and ours.

While it is a healthy step to allow the family boundary to become more permeable, it is crucial not to allow the boundary to become too permeable. The Samuels family had suffered the results of such a vulnerable boundary. Dennis, thirteen, and Richard, twelve, were brought in by Mr. and Mrs. Samuels for family therapy after Richard had defiantly erupted one night. No one had been able to control him until his father had wrapped his arms tightly around him and immobilized him. Mr. Samuels described Richard as "defiant, disobedient, mouths off, angry, sullen, having temper tantrums, withdrawn." Richard's brother, Dennis, was angry too, but his anger came out in more subtle, manipulative ways. He could be charming and deceptive at the same time.

This family had "parents" surrounding them. The grandparents watched closely for any misbehavior to critique and report to the boys' parents. Two aunts and one uncle checked every report card; they also regularly measured the boys, checking to see if they were getting too fat and notifying them any time an extra inch appeared. An older lady across the street checked the time Dennis and Richard arrived home after school, and a nearby elderly pastor checked on the parents to see if they were home on time, or at least what he determined to be the right time. The church youth group leaders were vigilant for the least infraction by these two boys. Even the principal at their small school seemed to have it in for them. Everywhere they went, it seemed parental eyes watched them—too many parental eyes, and yet not enough.

Although they themselves disliked the pressure, Connie and Lowell, the boys' actual parents, seemed helpless to do anything about all of the parents surrounding them. Neither of them had grown up with a healthy role model of what a parent needs to be. Both of them had mothers who were overprotective, and they knew they did not want that. So, for much of the time, they abdicated as parents and let the boys decide for themselves what they should do, knowing there were watching eyes around anyway.

Teenagers, however, need just one set of parents, not all of the others who may volunteer. They need parents who can be firm enough to set a boundary around the family. Lowell looked like he could be strong—he had been a linebacker for his college football team—but he had no idea how to carry out this role as a parent. Connie thought that if she were easy with the boys, they would not be bothered by all of the watchful eyes around them. She was wrong. They desperately needed and wanted parents who could parent them respectfully with a grace-oriented approach and with their full attention. Firm boundaries, like stakes for growing plants, provide a strong home base for young teens to grow. Parenting within a firm yet permeable boundary with grace creates a garden environment where your middle schooler can blossom.

PROTECTING YOUR FAMILY THROUGH FLEXIBILITY

A rigid, dried-up stick breaks more easily than a pliable green branch. An ice cube breaks apart when it hits the tile floor; spilled water still runs together. Likewise, a rigid family is more easily distressed than a flexible one. A rigid family is one that is unable or unwilling to make changes in its structure and rules and roles in order to meet changing developmental needs and situations.

Tom Cole fathered his family with an iron fist. When the children were young, his authoritarian stance, although not ideal, was tolerable. His own father had abandoned the family, and Tom had determined to do everything he could to keep his own family close together. His young children were not permitted to play with the neighborhood children after school. His wife had dinner on the table at five o'clock every night, not a minute late. He taught and guided by decree, and his rules had immediate punishments for violations. Everyone knew he was to be obeyed.

Then, when Matt Cole entered the seventh grade, he began to observe that other families were not like his. When he asked questions, his father neither listened nor cared, smug in the satisfaction that his way was the correct way to raise children. By the middle of eighth grade, Matt was sneaking around school, smoking and making connections to try some marijuana. By tenth grade, he was sexually active, using drugs and drinking to the point of intoxication weekly; his grades were failing. Matt had collided with a rigid family structure designed, mistakenly, to protect him, and he was headed for disaster.

Another family, the Chase family, was rigidly structured in a very different way. Sonja was overly involved with her daughters, vicariously living through them. She kept her husband at bay by telling the girls that he would be furious if he knew what they were involved in and telling her husband that the girls were terrified of him. Her marriage had little affection or genuine warmth. Her husband had grown up without sisters and did not have a clue how to relate to "these women." Although the atmosphere in the family was a little warmer than in the Cole family, the rigidity was equal. The crisis came when the Chase's oldest daughter, Casey, was in eighth grade. Although appearing perfect in all outward ways, she was seriously depressed and became bulimic.

The more rigid a family is, the more inward or outward rebellion parents can expect in their teenagers, including drug use. Most families of young teen substance abusers seem to have difficulty adapting to change. Research studies found that having a flexible family often reduces the risk of teen substance abuse. These researchers defined flexibility as the ability of families to change how they relate as the kids grow older and as they have to deal with new situations. Rather than forcing sameness, flexibility encourages change and growth.

Flexibility in the family allows the family to relate to the middle schooler according to his style of learning and moral reasoning development. According to moral development researcher Kohlberg, young children are basically motivated and taught by reward and punishment, a rather black and white type of thinking.[7] Young teenagers are influenced and motivated by relationship, societal rules, and role modeling, a more flexible type of thinking. As professors Issler and Habermas state, "Effective teaching is accomplished through—not despite—the needs and characteristics of our students; it requires the skill of knowing how students learn the material best."[8] We are not only parents of children, but also parents of students, students who are studying us to see what we are modeling!

A flexible family is one that believes these statements and tries to live them out:

- It is okay to have and state opinions.

- We can help and encourage each other to think for ourselves.

- Anger is okay and can be expressed appropriately in this family.

- Parents can say no without making an enemy.

- Age-appropriate differences are respected here.

- We listen to each other and do not make snap decisions.

- If the way we used to handle this issue no longer works, we will find a new and better way.

To develop flexibility in a family where there is none initially can be a little painful, and it always requires much repeated practice. Jeff, the son of family friends, is scheduled to have knee surgery due to a sports injury. During the surgery, doctors will cut and reattach the ligament to a higher, different position on the knee, stretching the ligament very tightly. The only way Jeff can then regain full use of his knee with a free range of motion is by going daily for physical therapy. There, slowly and gradually, the ligament will be stretched to become more flexible. Jeff has been told that the first few days will be extremely painful and that the therapy he will have to do will be time-consuming and tedious. But Jeff is an athlete who loves playing sports and working out, and he is willing to pay the cost. He feels too constrained by the limited movement of his knee as it is now. Similarly, when the range of movement within a family is too limited and flexibility needs to be introduced, the immediate cost can seem high, but the long-term benefits will be well worth it.

PRACTICE TIPS FOR SURVIVAL AND SUCCESS

1. Adopt this rule if you do not have it already: Everyone will knock and wait for an answer before entering another person's bedroom.

2. Another rule: We will always get permission from the owner before borrowing clothes or other personal things.

3. Practice allowing your children to disagree with you without cutting them off. Allow them to say: "I'm angry with you," and "No, I disagree with you."

4. Remember, you are responsible for your behavior as a parent! For guidelines, reflect on these qualities: love, joy, peace, patience, kindness, goodness, faithfulness, gentleness, and self-control. Run a quick checklist with yourself, asking, *Am I demonstrating these traits?*

   Keep in mind that the plank/speck principle applies to parent-child relationships. Concentrating on a teen's negative attitude or rudeness without first dealing with our own negative attitudes and rudeness will help no one.

5. Read *Boundaries* by Henry Cloud and John Townsend and *Boundaries for Kids,* also by Cloud and Townsend, for a deeper understanding of relational boundaries and their importance.

6. As you think about building the best kind of family boundaries try these ideas:

   - Discuss together the question, What is it that makes our family special?

   - Together, plan activities that you can do as a family. With teens, you will not be able to do this as frequently as before, and it is even more important now to ask for their input and find a way to incorporate it into decisions.[9]

7. Think *balance* as you communicate. One side of the scale is rigidity, and the other side is passivity/chaos. First, ask yourself, *Am I in balance?* If you are, you will be feeling calm inside as you show respect both for yourself and for the child you are talking with. If you are not in balance, calm down first, and you will find that you can be more thoughtful and creative in your response.

4
SECRET #4:
TURN DOWN THE HEAT

USE NEGOTIATION TO RESOLVE CONFLICT

Devon's family demonstrates that negotiation must begin between the parents. His father called to set an appointment for family therapy three weeks after Devon, a seventh grader, swallowed thirty aspirin and then told his mother.

As a young child, Devon seemed to have an unusual ability to concoct imaginative, intricate stories in an attempt to avoid homework, to avoid reporting grades to his parents (he *accidentally* left them in his jeans pocket when he washed his jeans), to "explain" why he shot a BB gun at the boxes in the garage. Three years before I met him, he began having gastrointestinal problems and hyperventilating at times, and neither of these problems were found to have physical causes. Jerry, his older brother, had problems sleeping, often lying awake for hours at a time. Their father, Jim, had been clinically depressed but now was feeling better. Devon himself had been depressed for five months. As we talked, a patterned undercurrent of this family emerged. Strong values and governing principles conflicted, creating a deadly undertow.

In front of a stretch of ocean near Ensenada, Mexico, beachfront signs warn, "Danger! Do not swim here!" Devon's family received similar signs which said, "Be careful! It's dangerous to live here." The danger zone in the stretch of water south of Ensenada is the result of two crosscurrents that collide with each other at right angles. You can see the rippled gridwork of the currents in the sand as you approach the area. While one current alone would not pose much of a problem, the two currents coming from different angles create a powerful undertow that could suck a swimmer into its turmoil and then out to sea.

In Devon's family, the crosscurrents emanated from the strongly maintained individual styles of the parents. Jim had an extreme need for peace at any cost, while his wife, Shelley, needed order in the home at any cost. Shelley was more than willing to sacrifice peace to get order, and Jim would happily surrender order to get peace. Shelley frequently screamed at the children to clean their rooms. Jim, however, avoided supervising the kids in an effort to keep things harmonious.

Jim and Shelley had never learned to resolve the conflict between them. Each was angry with the other for preventing his or her own needs from being met. Although the two genuinely loved each other, there was no sense of affection and play between them. Neither came from a family with healthy communication skills. Jim's family never expressed anger directly but held it inside where it sometimes erupted into an ulcer. They were highly critical, too, and to this day, continue to "put him down," in his words. Long before he married, Jim had determined that he would believe his children, not be judgmental of them, and protect them from others who were. Shelley, on the other hand, came from a family that valued order and timeliness as if they were moral virtues. Her kids described her as a "policeman" and as "too neat and too strict." Even she described herself as "too tight on obedience." Everyone agreed that she was the rigid one and Dad was the soft one.

Neither Shelley's nor Jim's basic ideas and values were invalid. In fact, had they been able to negotiate and integrate them with a degree of flexibility and lightheartedness, the family would have benefited. But that takes communication from the heart, being vulnerable with each other in order to uncover what is behind the values, and being willing to listen to each other without being defensive. Jim and Shelley did not have these skills, so they ignored the danger signals, stagnating in their well-meaning attempts to pass on what they had learned. Jerry and Devon wanted to be loyal to both of their parents and, as a result, felt caught in a web of helplessness. Devon's lying became an outward manifestation of the lie he felt he was living in this deadly zone, wanting but failing to be the son he thought he *should* be.

Parents who hold differing strong values, styles, or views must learn to communicate clearly and compassionately between themselves. If they do not accomplish the step of negotiating as partners, the results could be grim for their children—they may polarize to one of the parents' styles; they may become depressed; or they may act out in rebellion.

POOR NEGOTIATION BRINGS EMOTIONAL DISTRESS

Family psychiatrist Dr. Walt Kempler once declared that conflict resolution is to healthy family living what gastric juice is to digestion.[1] Without gastric juice, digestion and assimilation would never occur. Without good negotiation/conflict resolution skills a family is unable to solve problems and integrate individual differences, and, therefore, the family stagnates.

Maria's family never discusses anything that has potential for conflict. Bernie, her dad, has strong, opinionated ideas on just about everything, and his shaming silences when someone disagrees with him keep many topics out of discussion. Rather than ask if she can stay for the dance after the basketball game, Maria just lingers an hour before calling him to pick her up. Bernie will not talk to her about being late; he just fumes quietly and complains to her mother, blaming her for not having Maria under more control. This family avoids conflict but carries underlying anger and frustration. Bernie has an ulcer, and his wife has continual headaches.

Danny's family, on the other hand, wants to talk or yell about everything. His father's rage used to be frightening; now Danny has decided he has had enough and he fights back. When his dad threatens him with a month of grounding if he is even ten minutes late, Danny yells back, "You can't make me. Just try it!" Later when he arrives home twenty minutes late, his father grabs him by the shoulder, throws him into a chair, and wonders why Danny talks back to him. This family's conversations are filled with blaming, accusation, and "You make me so angry!" statements. The family members seem to thrive on conflict for entertainment as they hurl anger, but they rarely solve any problems. As with any middle schooler who lives with angry confrontations, Danny's emotional adjustment is hindered.

POSITIVE NEGOTIATION BRINGS CONSTRUCTIVE CHANGE

Susana's family understands that people make mistakes and get angry and that you can have good ideas no matter what age you are. Her parents are more interested in developing responsibility than resentment in their children. They seem to grasp intuitively what recent studies have shown—that angry speech will provoke anger and antagonism in others.[2] When Susana came home from the game twenty minutes later than the agreed-upon time, her mother and father put into effect a consequence already decided; she would have to come home twenty minutes early from the next event she attended. Susana knew what the consequence would be because she and her parents had already discussed it together. Her parents had even asked her to list out some consequences that she thought would be good ones for someone her age.

Susana's family understands how to be flexible and negotiate. Even though her parents may feel angry, they know that a reactive response can be ineffective and counterproductive. They would likely agree with the approach business owner and manager Sheldon Bowles describes using with an employee.[3] Watching a worker at one of his gas stations as she asked the fill 'er up? question, he noticed that she did everything right, except she forgot—horrors!—to wash the windshield. He says,

> I was livid, angry. My instinct was to go over there and chew her out. But I figured that was the wrong thing to do. So I took

a five dollar bill out of my wallet, cupped it in my hand, and went over to the employee. I told her she was doing a great job, that she had done the greeting and asked the question right. I gave her the five. And then in shock, she said, "Oh my gosh, I forgot to wash the windshield." And she put that right immediately and never forgot to do it [again]. Had I just been angry, I would have alienated her, she might have quit, and nothing would have been gained.

Bowles was successful in getting the type of response he wanted by being flexible and thinking about how to have a positive impact on this woman.

Middle school principal Lance Otis said that in most of the altercations at their school, "the kids do not have the skills to negotiate their way, to think their way through a confrontation, to bring it to a successful end." He illustrated his point this way: "If I come up and put my hand on your head and push down, you're going to push back. That's our nature. We need to override that by being peacemakers." Families can and should be the context in which kids learn the negotiation skills that will help them solve problems for the rest of their lives.

MODELING NEGOTIATION SKILLS

Healthy families negotiate best when the parents respect each other and can alternate smoothly, partnering as a loving team. This attitude of teamwork is often reflected in the way parents set up the broad outlines of their life, taking turns making personal and professional sacrifices at times. Brad's father's job is less demanding than his mother's. His work is done by 3:00 P.M., so he plans the menus and cooks the dinners. Both of Sara's parents have challenging professional careers. Sara's mother cut her work hours to one-half time, so she could be home during the afternoons and evenings. Her father loves to cook, but her mother now has more time, so she shops and cooks most of the meals. When Sara is out of high school, her mother plans to return to work full-time.

Divorced parents can model negotiation in the way they help

their kids sort out conflicting feelings of loyalty towards warring parents. Brandon, a confused sixth-grade son from a newly divorced family told his father, Don, "Dad, I don't know who I'm supposed to side with."

His father's wise response was this: "You don't have to side with either one of us. When you're with Mom, you can enjoy being with Mom, and when you're with me, you can have fun being with me."

Don went on, "You have a best friend, Kevin. Suppose one day you're going to introduce him to me. But first you decide to tell me that he's really a jerk, not nice, tries to hurt people, and I won't like him. Now what should I do? Should I just listen to you and believe automatically what you say, or should I decide to think for myself and see what I think about him?"

Brandon answered, "Okay, Dad, I see. I guess you should think for yourself."

Don, who was committed to remaining silent about Brandon's mother's parenting style, continued, "It's the same way with Mom and me. I'm sure you'll hear some really bad things about me and maybe some bad things about Mom, but I hope you can think for yourself and figure out what to do."

IDEAS FOR PARENTS FROM A SUPER NEGOTIATOR

Bill Richardson is a man known for his abilities in talking tyrant dictators into agreements with the U.S.A. As a former U.S. Congressman and the U.S. Representative to the United Nations, Richardson has become a favorite political troubleshooter. He has negotiated with Fidel Castro, Saddam Hussein, and Mobutu Sese Seko. While you know your middle school children are not dictators or tyrants, there may be days when you wonder about that. Richardson's ideas, taken from an interview with him, will prove helpful to you in your negotiating as well as serve as lessons for your young teens on how to negotiate in their world.[4]

First, Richardson says, "You have to connect personally with the individual with whom you are negotiating." Richardson found that referring to a time of previous good negotiation established a connection; other times he would make a cultural connection, and other times a religious connection. He comments, "You try to get into their minds and make them feel comfortable with you—that you're a person of trust and a person with respect."

In this fashion, negotiation between a parent and a middle schooler might sound like this:

> Father to Todd: Remember how we resolved our differences about your demanding to add basketball to extend your school day? When you talked to me calmly and told me how much you wanted to play on the team, I changed my schedule so I could pick you up later three days a week.

> Todd: Oh, yeah. When I found out how hard it was for you to make those kinds of changes, I said I'd try to get a ride with Sam's mom for the other two days. That worked.

> Father: We were starting to get kind of angry at each other just now. I'd like to try to resolve it like we did before and really listen to each other.

Negotiator Richardson's friendliness comes in handy when some world leaders are resistant. He explains:

> You have to be a human being. You cannot be arrogant or condescending. My nature is open and gregarious. I kid people. And it works. If you treat each individual with respect, each nation with dignity, you can get a lot further than trying to muscle them.

Similarly, when a young teen is standing his ground, trying to muscle him will hurt both of you.

For extreme situations where friendliness and cooperation never come from the opponent, for example with a dictator like Saddam Hussein, Richardson takes a firmer stand: "You don't show any fatigue. You can't show weakness." With Castro, Richardson finally stated, "Look, it's probably best that I go home. You're not giving me anything, and I'm going to have to announce that I went back empty-handed, and I don't think that is in your interest." True negotiating then began.

Even when a young teen has become sullen, resistant, and somewhat hostile, showing respect and appealing to his best interest can help negotiation. This might sound like the following conversation:

> Mother to Kiet: Your science teacher left a message for me today. He said you've been rude and out of control all week in class. He wanted me to talk to you and then call him back.
>
> Kiet: I don't care about him. He's such a jerk. I'll do what I want. If he doesn't like it, he can kick me out of class.
>
> Mother: You're right, you're the only one who can control what you do. I will call him back and tell him there's nothing you're willing to change, but I don't think that is in your best interest.
>
> Kiet: Okay. I guess I could try to put up with him.

Richardson sometimes kidded with powerful leaders and found it opened up cooperation. Once, after he joked with North Koreans who were absolutely convinced they were right, they eventually softened their position. Humor can provide just the right response to an adamant middle schooler as well. Like a staunch country leader, Brooke, age twelve, came home from school with an agenda. All of her friends had navel rings, tongue rings, a pierced nose, or, at the very least, a tattoo on their leg. She alone, she declared, remained unaltered. A budding teen building her case with everyone behind her can be a formidable force. Brooke's mom had different ideas for her adornment and knew that a lighthearted approach often worked with her daughter. She responded:

> I understand that you really want a navel ring and that all of your friends have one. Not only is it not a good idea for you,

but it would be disastrous for me. The MUFFPO (Mothers United For Fashion Police Observation) would show up at my office and pierce my ear on the spot to show that I truly had a hole in my head. And how would I explain that one to my boss?

This type of playfulness only works to aid negotiation if it is not sarcastic, is natural and warm, and comes from a firm position.

SETTING THE STAGE FOR NEGOTIATION

How you think about yourself and your young teenager sets the stage for negotiation. If, as a parent, I sincerely believe that:

- parenting middle schoolers will be the most awful time of my life;

- only a young teen's strict adherence to my rigid rules will protect him against the wiles of the world;

- my competence and value as a parent will be totally judged by my young teen's behavior;

- I must win every power struggle with him; and

- all of this near-perfect parenting can be totally undermined by too much contact with his peers;

then all interactions with my middle schooler will take on a very serious, almost life-or-death quality. This is a guaranteed way to produce a rigid family structure that will be counterproductive to what I really wish to see happen in my teen's life. If, instead, I can view the teenage years as a challenge, a time when I will grow and change as much as my child, and if I can view my middle schooler as a young adolescent who is pretty level-headed most of the time and is cooperative when approached respectfully, my parenting approach can be both free and strong. It can move from control to learning along with my child while providing important parental guidance.

Being open to learning from a difficult situation is the opposite of trying to control a difficult situation. We try to control situations in order to protect ourselves from hurt, embarrassment, helplessness, and aloneness. When we choose to learn from a situation, we accept the responsibility of being flexible and of experiencing feelings without getting stuck and reacting. With that kind of attitude we can be truly open to seeing our young teens with new eyes. Eighth-grader Allison said this to me concerning what she wished parents understood about young teenagers: "Our lives are stressful, too, as well as theirs. Like for our age, school is just as stressful as a job. School is really hard for me. Put themselves in our shoes and realize our lives are just as stressful as theirs."

LIGHTENING UP

When I talk to my teenager, there are two messages going on at once: what I say to her and how I say it to her. How I say it to her will determine both how she interprets what I say and how open she will be to what I have to say. Lectures, anger, and serious intensity will normally elicit some outward compliance, but at the same time inward defensiveness and a low level of inner compliance. Parental lectures usually trigger this kind of inner dialogue for your teen: "Here he goes again, on his high horse. I wish he would just shut up. What does he think I am, an idiot? And I have to sit here pretending to listen. I hate this." To angry communications she might respond (internally): "What a jerk! He is so unfair. He thinks I'm not behaving. Look at who's really out of control! I hate it when he does this." Serious angry intensity provokes defensiveness and a strong desire to get away, like someone who has been cornered.

None of these communication styles produces what the parents really want to see in their child at a moment of conflict or in their long-term style of conflict resolution. Focusing on your demeanor and behavior, your teen concentrates on how outrageous and out of place your actions are as he tunes out what you have to say to him. For this reason, it makes perfect sense for you to focus on doing with your teens what *The One Minute Manager* suggests for the workplace: "Help (them) reach their full potential—Catch them doing something right."[5] And limit your reprimands to one minute, remembering that when those thirty to sixty seconds are over, they are over. Don't hold a grudge and remember to remind your teen how much you value her.

Beyond the relative ineffectiveness of lectures and intensity, there are good reasons for keeping a sense of lightheartedness. It communicates that life is not hopeless and neither is your teenager, that problems are frequently solvable, and that change can be welcomed rather than feared. Lightening up reduces defensiveness and replaces it with lowered tension and laughter, a sense of acceptance and connecting together, and an openness to cooperation. Joking or laughing together turns us away from a rigid focus on control that can actually prohibit solving the problem at hand.

Have you ever tried to solve the following problem?

Connect these nine dots with a connecting series of four line segments, keeping your pencil on the paper with no backtracking allowed.

```
    •   •   •

    •   •   •

    •   •   •
```

Our usual problem-solving method focuses on solving this puzzle within the area covered by the dots. It cannot be solved this way, however. To solve the problem, your vantage point has to go beyond the area, outside the usual arena of focus. Then the solution becomes very simple:

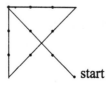

start

Similarly, areas of impasse in a family can frequently be resolved by looking beyond the usual parameters of control, such as setting limits and grounding. This allows room for creativity in problem solving, like the mother who appealed to the fashion police. Taking a lighthearted approach to life and using humor appropriately softens rigidity in a family's pattern of relating, allowing members to disentangle, step back, and take a fresh look at options. The more angles from which you can view a problem, the easier it is to resolve in an effective way.

The negotiation you are working on can feel frightening and dangerous, especially if the changes your middle schooler clamors for seem to threaten your identity. Instead, you can develop the perspective that the middle school years (two to three years depending on where you live) really only last about 10 percent of the entire span of time he will be living with you in the same house, and during that time you probably will not be able to fully understand him anyway, so why not learn to smile a little along the way? Smiling is contagious and helps create a positive atmosphere. If marriage (a relationship between two mature adults) requires a 5 to 1 ratio of positive to negative interchanges to survive happily over time,[6] what do you think the necessary ratio would be for the parent-to-young-teen relationship (in which at least one of the participants is not a mature adult) to flourish? Most likely it would be at least a 5 to 1 ratio. Bringing humor into your interactions boosts the positive side and has the additional benefit of increasing your creative problem solving abilities.

LEARNING TO APOLOGIZE

Youth pastor Steve Inrig thinks learning how to apologize is a valuable skill for enhancing negotiation between parents and middle school kids. He says,

> When a parent makes a mistake and is able to go to the kid and say, "I was wrong and I'm sorry," the child learns grace from the parent. But there's also a mutuality about this relationship. We're not just a father telling a son what to do. We're

two people working together towards a goal of health and maturity, and I, the parent, haven't gotten there. The kids already know that. You might as well just bring it out into the open."

What is an apology and why does it help negotiation? An apology is a repair tactic to restore relationship.[7] When a parent wrongs a child, the child is wounded, bent over with a load of shame dumped on him by the parent—"You're such an irresponsible kid." A good apology returns shame from the wounded to the original owner, the wounder. A good apology is specific and timely and restores a sense of power and worth to the wronged—"I'm sorry. I'm the one who's being irresponsible with how I talk to you. I didn't mean to hurt you. I was wrong to do that." After this, respectful negotiation can resume.

Some types of apologies do not work to restore relationship nor do they enhance negotiation. "I'm sorry if I hurt you," for example, does not acknowledge fault or take responsibility for causing hurt. "I need you to forgive me right now" demands forgiveness without allowing time for the wounded one to heal. Overapologizing does not work either—a long apology for a minor offense is an attempt to restore self-respect, not an attempt to own our wrongdoing and hence relieve the false blame placed on our child.

Three other barriers to the success of an apology include: pride, "I didn't really do anything wrong"; selfishness replacing concern for the wounded party, "I'm sorry you're upset with me"; and minimization, "I didn't think it was any big deal anyway."

Good apologies are taught best by modeling. As a parent, you can say to a middle school child, "I'm sorry I embarrassed you by butting into your conversation. I was wrong to think that my agenda was more important than yours." With a good model your child will become more natural with her apologies to you and to her friends.

USING STRATEGIES FOR NEGOTIATION

Strategies for negotiation can be taught and practiced. Start with healthy self-respect combined with respect for the opposition.

STRATEGY #1: THE MAGIC FORMULA

Wexler teaches groups of adolescents how to negotiate. He uses Dr. John Parker's formula, which can work wonders when used consistently.[8] Again, parents need to model this as well as guide kids in using it. The Magic Formula has three parts: the Stroke, the "I" Message, and the Detective.

Here are examples of its use by both a parent and a young teen:

> Parent to Middle Schooler: (The Stroke) I appreciate how you're growing in independence and wanting to make more decisions for yourself.
>
> (The "I" Message) I'd like for you to finish all of your homework this week before you go to Sam's on Saturday.
>
> (The Detective) What needs to happen so that I don't have to remind you and it just gets done?
>
> Middle Schooler to Parent: (The Stroke) I'm glad you care about me, Dad. You must worry about me.
>
> (The "I" Message) I'd like to stay after school and play basketball and then go to Gilli's house. I'd be coming home about three hours later than usual.
>
> (The Detective) What can I do to show you that I'm ready to handle this? What can I do to build your trust?

STRATEGY # 2: FAIR NEGOTIATION

Negotiation becomes difficult when family members feel attacked, criticized, and left out. Good negotiators never demean or criticize others; they focus their efforts on the specific problem to be solved. Parents can use these principles for fair negotiation and teach their middle school children to use them as well:

1. State the problem.

2. Be specific and focus on today.

3. Address the problem. No attacks on people allowed.

4. Listen to each other with an open mind.

5. Show respect to each other by calmly expressing and listening to feelings.

6. Decide to take responsibility for your actions (even if your part was small).

FACING PROBLEMS YOU CANNOT RESOLVE

Every family has problems that cannot be resolved. Parents, as well as young teens, have some style differences that will not change much. Research tells us that what is important about these unresolvable problems is that we are able to keep the conversation open about them. Parents like Jim and Shelley at the beginning of this chapter may never fully agree with each other, but they can learn to be more lighthearted and have friendly discussions about their differences.

CREATING FAMILY TIMES TO WORK ON NEGOTIATION

When Geoffrey was twelve years old, he greeted his mom after school with the comment, "I wonder if God maybe isn't real." Shocked, his mother reacted and said, "Of course He's real, and we won't talk about that any more." Today, Geoffrey is a young adult who has jettisoned his faith. His mother did not understand that banning questions never eliminates the doubt and uncertainty. Prohibition of such intellectual grappling only serves to say, What you ask frightens me. To resist open discussion is to invite a later repudiation of what you are trying to protect.

If you have not done so already, start the practice of having a regular family time to discuss issues, check in on feelings, and give spiritual guidance. (The Tips section at the end of the chapter has more ideas for your family times.) Your eighth grader may come home from school one day and say, "Well, Dad, I do believe in abortion. You just can't tell a woman what to do with her body." The father who says, "Well, Susie, you know what I think. I'm disappointed in you. You show a lack of morals. I don't want to talk about this any more," may sound kind. His opinionated daughter, however, may respond to this by simply burying not only the questions she wanted answered but also her trust in her father. She then builds her case silently, and, with no safe arena to discuss and hear wisdom, her case solidifies. Contrast this with the father who responds, "It sounds like you have some pretty strong feelings about this. Tell me more." As this daughter expresses her feelings and feels heard, not condemned, she will be freed to think more clearly and to be open to what you have to say.

Without attention and treatment, problems in the middle school years can spread like cancer. Work to keep feelings and concerns manageable by welcoming them as topics for friendly discussion in your family times. Your middle schooler benefits by learning how to express himself, listen to others, and negotiate differences. You and your family benefit from a sense of connection and warmth as you talk together.

- Average size of problem
  detected at weekly family meetings.

 Average size of problem
detected when there are no
family meetings in place.

PRACTICE TIPS FOR SURVIVAL AND SUCCESS
Negotiating is a skill requiring much practice. Keep after it; the

results for your family are worth all the effort. Here are some ideas.

1. Plan a special family meal together. Have everyone contribute ideas. Decide on menu, dishes to use, placemats, candles, and location (dining room, kitchen, picnic blanket in the backyard). Everyone needs to agree with the final choices. (This can be more difficult than it sounds. When our children were younger, we tried to limit their sugar intake. One simple idea involved letting them have one box of junk-food cereal each year, but they had to agree on the choice. Some years they just could not decide and never got the cereal.) Buy the groceries, prepare the meal, and share it together.

2. Negotiation becomes easier when family members can clearly state what they want and need. Try this during a family time. To practice being clear, write down the following on a three-by-five card for each person:

    I think

    I want

    I need

    I wish

    I like

    I dream

Give each person a card. Take turns or go popcorn fashion (randomly), completing the sentence. You can do this on general topics or specific topics (such as a family outing, homework, friends, church). Since there are no right or wrong ways to complete the sentences, all responses are okay.

3. Teach and practice the Say, Ask rule: "I want to go shopping.

What do you want?" Guessing and assuming what another person wants only hampers negotiation.

4. Set up some simple ways of resolving small disagreements. For example: With one piece of pie left, one person divides it, and the other one (or ones) chooses first.

5. Choose to focus more on what you can do than on what you cannot do.

6. When all else fails, try something different. (Remember that one of the definitions of insanity is doing the same thing over and over and expecting different results.) If one technique keeps failing, try a new one.

7. Focus on win-win solutions, where both sides win.

8. Discuss some well-known apologies. Which of these are good apologies that would aid negotiation?

   ■ The prodigal son's apology in Luke 15:11-32.

   ■ F. W. de Klerk's apology in 1993 to South Africans for his political party's introduction and maintenance of apartheid: "It was not our intention to deprive people of their rights and to cause misery, but eventually apartheid led to just that. Insofar as that occurred, we deeply regret it. Deep regret goes further than just saying you are sorry. Deep regret says that if I could turn the clock back, and if I could do anything about it, I would have liked to have avoided it."
   Regarding their new policy de Klerk said, "It is a statement that we have broken with that which was wrong in the past and are not afraid to say we are deeply sorry that our past policies were wrong."[9]

   ■ Mike Tyson's apology, as reported in the *Las Vegas Review Journal*, 1 July 1997, to Evander Holyfield after twice intentionally biting his ear during a prize fight: "I apologize to the world, to my family, and to the Nevada State Athletic Commission . . . [everyone except Evander Holyfield]. I just snapped and did what many athletes have done and paid the price for." To Evander he said, "I am sorry . . . When you butted in that first round, accidentally or not, I snapped in reaction, and the rest is history." (Note the minimization and overapologizing combined.)

- Senator Edward M. Kennedy of Massachusetts in a TV address after the 1969 tragedy in Chappaquiddick when he drove off a bridge while drinking, killling his female companion: "The car that I was driving went off a narrow bridge." (Note his avoidance of personal responsibility for the accident.)

Discuss what you as a family can learn from these apologies. Role play scenarios where an apology is needed.

9. Brainstorm and list fouls for family negotiation. Create a Forbidden sign (circle with a diagonal slash) and write these outlawed expressions on it. Sample items:

   Name calling
   Blaming each other
   Making excuses
   Making threats
   Bringing up the past
   Hitting and pushing and throwing things

5
SECRET #5:
SHARE POWER
SHOW RESPECT AND
GIVE FREEDOM

Several years ago, Captain John Testrake spoke to a class I attended. Testrake was the pilot for the TWA jet that was hijacked and rerouted to Lebanon on June 14, 1985. Along with other crew members and many of the passengers, he was held hostage inside the jet for two weeks as it sat on the airport tarmac. As he spoke of the ordeal, he asked if any in the audience knew why hijackers hijack. Since there were no responses, he explained, "Hijackers hijack because they don't have any real power."

A remarkable similarity exists between some young teenagers and hijackers—when teenagers have no power, they may choose to hijack the family in an effort to gain the power to be heard and taken seriously. Ivan, fourteen, is one example. One night at 2:00 A.M. he slipped out his bedroom window, pushed the new family car down the driveway into the street, turned the engine on, and drove to pick up a waiting friend. From there, the boys proceeded to another area of town, met other friends, and began drag racing down the streets. Within minutes the family car was totaled; the shocked boys were driven by police to the station to write a report and call their parents. Mission accomplished, hijacking completed: the family's main source of transportation had just been demolished.

Ivan's parents had been arguing heatedly for months about

whether the family should move, and no one had ever asked Ivan what he thought. It seemed as if they did not care. The family had moved too many times, and Ivan was desperate to stay near his friends. He had no power in this family, however, and no way to get his parents to listen to him. So he hijacked the family. Now they knew without a doubt that something was seriously wrong. Like most young teenagers who hijack, Ivan did not consciously think about what he was doing; he reacted out of his anger and sense of helplessness, a more subconscious process.

Parents need to learn to ride out power struggles without fighting back. The trick is to behave like a swimmer being carried out to sea by a rip tide—when the tide reaches a certain point, it dissipates, and the swimmer can safely swim back to shore. Frightened swimmers who choose not to wait but to fight the current will exhaust themselves and probably drown. Frightened parents have also been known to drown.

All young teenagers need a sense of power and a source of appropriate attention, and they will find ways to get both if you as parents abdicate or minimize this responsibility. Sometimes a young teen may feel that her only power lies in her power to resist you or in her power to do things poorly. A middle school child can always win a power struggle by doing nothing. Both her need for attention and her need for adequate power can be met in a better way, though, as you respect her as a valuable person who has valid concerns and deserves to be listened to. How do you respect a young teenager? The same way you show respect for anyone else, as you make allowances for individual differences.

KNOWING OUR WORTH

Haim Ginott, who was eulogized by his adult stepdaughter as the most sensitive, caring man she had ever known, wrote, "We win our teen's attention when we listen with a third ear and respond with a sympathetic tongue. We win his heart when we express for him clearly what he said vaguely. We win respect when we are authentic, when our words fit our feelings."[1] To win respect in this way, by being authentic, you as a parent must first respect yourself.

You must know your worth and know the worth of your teenager. This story about a painting illustrates how such knowledge can change how you relate to each other.

Several years ago, we returned to France to show our children where they were born. While there, we bought an oil painting of a storefront scene in Paris from a street artist for four hundred francs (eight-five dollars at that time). Some years later when we redecorated, we decided our French painting did not go with our new color scheme, so under the bed it went, to collect dust.

When Michèle moved out to attend college, we redecorated her room and hung the dusted-off painting there. A year later when my cousin Bobby came to visit, he recognized the painting on the wall as a Pradzinsky. Unbeknownst to us, the artist had in recent years become famous; this painting was actually worth around ten thousand dollars. And we had had it under the bed gathering layers of dust! Of course, we began to treat the painting very differently, and with great care. I definitely did not stick it under the bed again. We began to think about how to reframe it and where to put it downstairs to show it off more.

Why the change in how we related to this piece of art? The reason was that its *worth* had changed in our eyes. Had it changed in and of itself? No. Its intrinsic value as a piece of canvas with some paint applied had not altered at all. How we viewed it had changed. It was now worth a great deal. How did its worth change? The president of Mitsubishi at that time had seen an exhibition of Pradzinsky's work in Tokyo, loved it, and bought the entire exhibit. The value of Pradzinsky's creations had escalated. Elite galleries had begun to carry his art. The paintings themselves had not changed. One man had declared their worth with his choice and with his purchase.

Another man, Jesus Christ, declared the worth of that moody middle schooler in your home when He paid the price of his life. That irritable teenager—the one welcomed as a newborn, delighted in as a toddler, enjoyed and endured as an energetic fifth grader— *that* teenager is the same person that Christ stated (rather emphatically by hanging on a cross) is worth more than anything you can ever buy, barter, or earn.

As parents, we need to first respect ourselves for who we are, people created in the image of God, and then respect our children for who they are, people created in the image of God. Then, as we treat each other as original masterpieces of great worth, we can begin to listen and talk in a new way.

MODELING ATTITUDES TOWARD WORTH

Sam and June came to my office one day in utter exasperation. Their middle school son was openly belligerent at home, calling both of them unprintable names in a threatening way whenever his frustration level peaked. He was quite large, and they feared his mouthiness would become increasingly intimidating both to their other children and to themselves.

When the initial changes they made did not help to alter this dynamic, I asked if there was anyone else in the family who displayed this same menacing behavior. Reluctantly, they told of how Sam's father had treated his mother like this and how Sam, on occasion, would demonstrate the same intense and demeaning rage in his treatment of June. It seems that Sam modeled disrespect and a lack of worth and power to his family, and his son was returning the favor.

All of us probably can point to examples of the truth that what we model to our children is much more likely to be adopted by them as their own behavior than what we teach or tell them to do.

Several years ago, my husband and I spoke at a family retreat. While he spoke to the adults for one session, I had the task of speaking to the teenagers on the topic, How to Communicate Better with Your Parents. My own children, ages ten and twelve at that time, were in the audience. Halfway into my talk, as I was explaining a particular point, my daughter's hand shot up, and she boldly declared to me and to everyone else, "But Mom, you don't talk to us that way!"

After surviving my utter embarrassment and intense desire to magically disappear off the stage, I somehow recouped. Then, knowing that even in moments like these children need to be respected and valued, I asked Michèle if she would tell the group what, in her opinion, our family had done that *had* worked. She shared a few ideas we had successfully used (as I silently resolved to never again speak to an audience which included my own children). Michèle remembered and valued what her dad and I had done ourselves, not what we simply told her and her brother to do.

AVOIDING COMMUNICATION THAT UNDERMINES POWER

When I communicate with my children, I have choices of different postures from which to communicate. I can take a critical stance: "You are such a slob! Look at your room. Don't you know any better? Why are you such a pig?" Criticism of this sort invites one of three responses:

1. Dejection (giving up power)—"I'll never get it right."

2. Reaction/Rebellion (misguided attempt to regain power)— "Leave me alone. It's my room and I don't care what you think!"

3. Defensiveness (attack and retreat to regain a pseudo power)— "You wouldn't be able to do any better. I've been too busy."

Criticism attacks a sense of self and power in our young teens. By criticizing, we end up contributing to their emotional immaturity.

Second, I can communicate from an overly nurturing posture: "Honey, since you stayed up so late last night watching TV, let me clean up your room and do your science project for you." This stance provokes one of two responses:

1. Feigned Helplessness (the pampered child reaction)—"You're right, I just can't do it," he says as he takes another step on the descent to being an underfunctioner who begins to believe he is helpless to do all that life requires.

2. Reaction/Rebellion: "Just leave me alone! You always try to nose in on my things."

Communicating from an overly nurturing posture also contributes to our children's emotional immaturity.

Third, I can communicate from a hurt child posture: "You don't care about me. Nobody appreciates all that I do. If you did, you would clean your room better." This posture creates a guilt cloud over your young teen, and, since guilt feelings are always uncomfortable, she likely will respond with an angry, an anxious, or an avoidant response: "Give me a break!" or "Nothing I ever do is good enough" or "I'm going to my messy room."

Goleman, in his excellent book *Emotional Intelligence,* describes similar dynamics when he talks about "the three most common emotionally inept parenting styles," all of which eclipse healthy empowerment:[2]

- Style 1—"Ignoring feelings altogether," in which the parents treat the child's emotional upsets as a bother to them.

- Style 2—"Being too laissez-faire," in which parents either go along with whatever means a child chooses to handle his feelings or bribe the child to stop the feeling.

- Style 3—"Being contemptuous, showing no respect for how the child feels," in which parents disapprove and harshly criticize and even punish for emotional responses.

It is possible to avoid communicating in a style that undermines your teen's power. The key to this is respect.

SHOWING RESPECT FOR YOUR YOUNG TEEN

When we respect our middle schoolers, we are able to communicate in more of an adult fashion with them, and we help them solidify their inner sense of self. One summer day after my daughter's seventh-grade year was over, I moved aside some clothes and sat down on the floor of her room, right next to her bed. I was there at her invitation to sit and talk and help her clean up her room. I reached under the bed and pulled out what appeared to be a used lunch bag, but it still had something in it. Inside was a juicy something—an orange, which by now was rotten and half liquid. I caught myself starting to say something critical and then reminded myself I really should talk to her in the way I suggest to parents in my office every week. Glancing at her I said, "It looks like you didn't want to eat your lunch that day" (a descriptive comment that maintains respect, rather than a judgmental comment that destroys respect). She looked rather sheepish, reached out to take the bag, and responded, "Oops, I guess I'd better clean this up right away." She took the responsibility without feeling resentful, a result that frequently follows a respectful stance.

The same daughter at age ten surprised us one afternoon with her own version of a respectful conversation after some visiting friends left. Tim and Sarah had come over to talk with us because Tim was feeling devastated by a comment one of his professors had written on the comprehensive exam for his master's degree. At the bottom of the last page, after a lengthy essay response, the professor had written, "You are not a creative thinker!" Since Tim had wanted to continue on at an Ivy League school for his doctorate, this negative, judgmental comment was particularly crushing.

After he left, our daughter Michèle, who had overheard the conversation and noticed his dejected appearance, commented, "That teacher should have written, 'This paper does not show the creative thinking I know you are capable of.'" Even a ten-year-old can understand what a respectful interaction sounds like. When you as a parent communicate to your young teen in this way, you greatly increase the possibility that she will respond in a thoughtful way as well.

Showing respect to your young teen works by giving him power while maintaining your own power. No power struggles are needed. He knows that you will listen to him and consider what he has to say. Respectful attention defuses power struggles. Yesterday in my office, Darcy, an eighth grader, hurled names and accusations at her mother who had just criticized and laughed at her. Neither was showing respect. Minutes later, Darcy was softly telling how hurt and neglected she has felt. Her mother listened and responded warmly. The difference? Darcy's mother gave Darcy the power of knowing she would be heard by changing her own behavior to respect and listen to Darcy.

Shared power allows family members to express emotions such as anger openly. Even Scripture tells us that it is important to do so in commands such as, "Do not let the sun go down while you are still angry" (Ephesians 4:26). When a young teen feels respected, worthwhile, and powerful enough to do so, he can say: "I'm angry that we couldn't work out something so I could go to the dance," and not, "You never let me do anything." He can leave aside accusation as he chooses expression and communication.

Shared power and respect for feelings also benefits your individual teenager in her growth as a person. As you empower her by helping her learn how to manage her emotions, she grows in confidence, her curiosity ignites, she takes more initiative, her self-control improves, her ability to relate to others improves, she grows in her capacity to communicate, and she becomes a more cooperative person.

LAUGHING TO DEFUSE POWER STRUGGLES

Laughing with a child brings warmth and friendliness. It is almost impossible to laugh with someone you are angry at or with someone you want to distance yourself from. Our kids need to remember to laugh, too, and Principal Otis adds that it helps when kids can laugh at themselves. He sees this as part of learning "that everybody's a little goofy and zany" and so we should not put so much weight on what somebody else thinks. Otis uses this philosophy throughout the school day. He explained how important fairness is to these kids. When a middle school student protests innocence, he often asks, "How many times have you done something you didn't get caught for?" The answer typically is, "Lots."

"See," Otis answers, "I'm just getting you back for one of those," and this usually gets a smile.

Recently I had an appointment with the daughter of an Ivy League-educated mother with a Ph.D. The girl's grades had fallen miserably from *A*s and *B*s to *D*s and *F*s for the previous entire year. I have learned that most young teens in this predicament do not need lectures on studying or training in note taking. What they often need is the right nudge to jolt them out of their self-dug rut. And, while theirs is a serious problem, dealing with it too seriously can actually make the problem worse.

I proposed to this girl two possible theories. First, I said, perhaps getting low grades was her way of letting her parents know that she really would not be ready to go away for college in a few years, that she actually wanted to stay at home longer and be around her parents more. After a momentary startled look, she burst out laughing, saying "No, I'm sure that wasn't the reason." Then I suggested theory two, that perhaps getting poor grades was her way of being different from her mother (whom she considered to be stuffy and a little odd). When she acknowledged that this might be the reason, we were able to focus on ways she could be different from her mother without sabotaging herself. This, in effect, took grades and her study efforts out of the power struggle with her parents and gave her the freedom to work on them as something she was motivated to do for herself.

Vice Principal Judy Kissinger described a security officer at her school who often solved potential power struggle problems with her laughter: "Nancy laughed very easily. In a tense situation, this kid would have excuses that wouldn't have anything to do with the subject, and Nancy would just start laughing, and pretty soon I was laughing and the teen was laughing, saying, 'Okay, okay, I'll go to OCS'" [On Campus Suspension]. The security officer began the laughter that defused the crisis.

GIVING YOUR MIDDLE SCHOOLER FREEDOM TO FEEL

As a little girl, Michèle asked, "When I die and go to heaven, will my feelings go with me?" Her feelings were important to her, and they are equally important to the development of the identity of every middle school child. As one seventh grader, Samuel, who lost a best friend to leukemia, was given the security, space, and love to explore and express his feelings (within protective limits, of course), he could feel sad and cry without getting depressed. He learned that feelings are not bad or good in and of themselves. Feelings are neutral. They gain power over an individual's life when the individual, his parents, or others prevent him from expressing those feelings in appropriate ways.

Validating a child's feelings does not increase those feelings, nor does it exacerbate bad behavior. Rather it allows the child to sense that she is not bad for feeling a certain way. She then is able to feel the feeling and be understood; the feeling is contained, then released, and the child goes away feeling and thinking, "I am okay."

Please note: I am not talking about behavior here, just feelings. If your child is feeling angry and running around with a knife in his hand, that is *not* okay! Differentiate between the feeling and the behavior in your communication with your teen—"It's okay to feel angry, but it's not okay to throw your English book. When you feel that angry, I'd like you to come and tell me so that we can talk about it."

RESPONDING WHEN TRAUMA DAMAGES A SENSE OF POWER

According to Jane Middleton-Moz, "all children experience traumatic events of one kind or another before reaching the age of eighteen."[3] Parents cannot always protect their children from the traumatic events, but they can protect them from the traumatic effect on their self-esteem. How? By four simple steps:

1. Acknowledge the event. "That wreck was awful. You saw the car crumple and people bleeding."

2. Be supportive in word, tone, and action. Take time to listen with focused attention.

3. Validate the emotion. Let your child know that you understand what she is feeling and that it is okay to feel that feeling. "That was really scary. I felt so helpless."

4. Allow Time. Time alone will not heal, but time is needed for your child's emotions to recede and for him to make sense of this world where bad things can happen to good people.

PRACTICE TIPS FOR SURVIVAL AND SUCCESS

First, you need to accept that you cannot win a power struggle with an adolescent. Even if you keep upping the ante on power, they still can take the upper hand by running away, doing something impulsive and destructive, or even attempting suicide. Learn instead to *empower* your teen by respectful listening. Here are some suggestions:

1. Practice reflective listening. Listen to what your teen says. Repeat back to him in your words what you understand him to be saying. Then ask him if that is what he meant. Example:

   Middle Schooler: I hate my teacher!

   Parent: It sounds as though you really are angry at your teacher.

   Middle Schooler: Yeah, he's such a jerk.

   Parent: He really messed up today?

   Middle Schooler: He's so stupid. He said I had to do my outline all over again.

   Parent: He's making you redo your homework that you spent so much time on last night?

   Middle Schooler: Yeah. Well, actually I just have to redo part of it.

   Parent: Part of it?

   Middle Schooler: Oh, it probably won't take that long.

This kind of reflective listening entrusts your teen with the responsibility of seeing and then doing what he needs to do. Had you taken a high control approach instead, saying, "I don't want to hear you mouth off like that. Get to your room and do your homework the right way right now!" you likely would have had a sullen teen and a stormy night ahead. Reflective listening involves controlling not your teenager, but yourself.

2. Take turns. Let your kids take turns leading the family. A middle schooler can plan and prepare an evening meal, even if it is just pizza. Discuss it with her ahead of time so you can buy what she will need to cook. Let your young teen navigate on a trip. Teach her how to use the map and let her guide the way. One time Michèle led our family time by choosing the topic and how she wanted us to discuss it. She gave us a short talk on greed and then had us each write a poem about greed, read it, and discuss our thoughts. The experience gave her a sense of power as someone in the family we could learn from.

3. Practice. Ask your young teen what she thinks, wants, and feels. Discuss together how she can manage these thoughts, desires, and feelings. Seek out her opinion.

6
SECRET #6:
MATCH YOUR WALK
AND YOUR TALK

LIVE YOUR SPIRITUAL VALUES ON A DAILY BASIS

In a scene in the first Superman movie, Superman assures Lois Lane that she is safe since he has caught her falling off a tall building. She replies that she knows Superman is holding her, but she asks, "Who is holding you?"

In the early years, your child may have been content with the knowledge that you as parents were holding him. During the early teen years, though, he wants to know who or what is holding you. If he feels safe in the security of your love, he probably will question you about how you know what you do about God. He needs the freedom to ask and to find answers, and he needs the reminder and assurance that his questioning does not threaten God.

Family research tells us that the healthiest families have strong spiritual values giving them hope, trust, and meaning when life is overwhelming. One recent study reported that when the family placed a high level of importance on religion and prayer, those resources helped protect seventh and eighth graders against alcohol use.[1] When spiritual values are not just talked about occasionally, but interwoven into daily life, families are like the houses built not on sand but on solid rock.

WHAT ARE WE PRACTICING AS PARENTS?

After working three years with middle school kids in his church, youth pastor Steve Inrig says, "People who are most effective in impressing godly values into the lives of their kids are people who practice those godly values themselves." He tells about a father who together with his wife decided to raise their kids with some religious influence. When the twelve-year-old daughter decided to accept Christ, the father, at forty years of age, did the same. Inrig says,

> If the principles aren't lived by, then those won't be passed on to kids. If they're lived by, they're passed sometimes without even having to declare, "Hey, this is a biblical principle." It becomes something that is caught by a kid, and they wouldn't be able to say, "Well this is from James 3." They'd be able to say, "I just saw my dad do this."
>
> Applying the principles in daily life speaks louder than words when it comes to family relationships. As Inrig explains, "Husbands, love your wives" is a biblical principle that is better passed on not by telling your kids but by practicing it.

Inrig gave an example of how his father had worked biblical principles into his family life during the growing up years:

> I remember what my dad did one time when we were watching a movie that had some nudity in it. The movie had some value, so instead of turning it off, he asked afterwards, "Now tell me how you feel about the fact that that woman was naked in front of millions of people who watched this movie, and what do you think God has to say about that?"

Parents who demonstrate and explain spiritual principles by how they live and treat people are always more effective than parents who only talk about the principles.

HOW ARE WE TREATING OUR KIDS?

Following is a slight paraphrase of 1 Corinthians 13:

> If I speak in the lingo of my young teens and can woo crowds of their friends while dressing young to fit in and don't have love, my words mean nothing.
>
> If I answer a telephone call for my kids with "Don't you know how late it is?! What kind of an irresponsible jerk are you?" and then remind them daily of their no-good friends, I am only a vibrating gong left over from the *Gong Show*.
>
> If I keep a list of my kids' mistakes so that I am never at a loss for grudges to justify my points, if I pretend respect but exude no love, I am a self-righteous fake and my teen will know it.

Giving the image of respect without genuinely felt love will hit your teen's ears like the bongs and clangs of gongs and cymbals. It is almost impossible to maintain a respectful attitude toward your young teen unless love is the basis. This 1 Corinthians 13 love—the patient, kind love that is not self-seeking, is not easily angered, and does not keep a record of wrongs—comes only from above. Only when we as parents learn to integrate God's love in our lives, can we hope to manifest this kind of respect for our moody, sarcastic middle schoolers.

The original version of the scripture paragraphs above goes on to explain that "when I became an adult, I put an end to childish ways" (NRSV). Just because my young teen still talks, thinks, or reasons like a child at times is no justification for me to do the same in reaction to her. Instead, because of God's love for me and in me, I can relate to her as an adult. Love truly is "the most excellent way" (1 Corinthians 12:31).

USING HUMOR TO INVITE PARTICIPATION

Youth Pastor Inrig explains why he thinks humor is important when communicating spiritual values for this age group:

> We want kids to come and have fun, partly because we take life, ourselves, important issues, and God sometimes far too seriously. There's room for humor and there's room for laughing. Humor breaks down walls that not a lot of other things can. I also think that humor builds memories. Families that laugh together remember those times and can say, "Oh, do you remember when you did this and we just laughed." And I think allowing for the fact that kids aren't adults means that you promote fun . . . we really try and do crazy things in our group so that our kids feel this is a safe place to have a good time.

A light-hearted approach with spiritual lessons helps as you navigate the changes your child goes through as he grows from a young child to a middle schooler. How a twelve-year-old thinks about spiritual things is different from how a ten-year-old thinks. At ten, Kristopher asked me if I knew what the fastest speed in the world was. "Spirit speed," he replied to my ignorance, "because in less than the blinking of an eye you'll be with Jesus when you die." A ten-year-old sees the world freshly and simply. Contrast that with a twelve-year-old whose hormones have kicked in. This young teen revealed her changing focus as she wrote this practice note to memorize a verse from Scripture:

> Psalm 19:14
> Let the words of my mouth and the thoughts of my heart, Let the words of my mouth and the thoughts of my heart. Let the words of my mouth & the thoughts of my heeeart be pleasing Lord to yoooouuuu.

Let the words of my mouth and the thoughts of my heart, let

the words of my mouth and the thoughts of my heart Let the words of my mouth and the thoughts of my heart, be pleasing lord to you.

I ♥

Scott
4-ever

WHAT DOES GOD SAY THAT COULD HELP US PARENT MIDDLE SCHOOLERS?

Several years ago, I bought a red Dodge Stealth. Ten weeks later, when the car had some problems, I did not pull out our lawnmower manual to see what was wrong. I opened up the Dodge Stealth manual because I knew that the same people who designed and manufactured that car wrote the manual.

If with something as replaceable as a car we follow custom-designed instructions and spend a load of money on repairs and upkeep, why do we stumble about with our families and children? The maker of these children—God, our heavenly Father—has written about their care in his instruction book:

- "We who are strong ought to bear with the failings of the weak and not to please ourselves" (Romans 15:1). Parents need to be true adults who can stand firm and loving while guiding their flailing changelings.

- "Love is patient, love is kind. . . . It is not rude, it is not self-seeking, it is not easily angered, it keeps no record of wrongs. . . . It always protects, always trusts, always hopes, always perseveres. Love never fails" (1 Corinthians 13: 4-8). Ouch! Was this really meant to include the parents of middle school kids? Does this mean that I should not be rude to my young teen? That I ought to watch my irritation level? That I need to deal with situations in the present without holding grudges?

- "The Father of compassion and the God of all comfort, who comforts us" (2 Corinthians 1: 3-4). The writer of Corinthians must have known about middle school kids and what we parents need.

- "How can this be?" (John 3). Just as Jesus lovingly and gently responded to Nicodemus's repetitions of this question, so we can respond to our children's never-ending "Why?" and "Why can't I?"

- "Will you give me a drink?" (John 4). We can learn from how Jesus dealt with wayward people. Jesus communicated respectfully to the Samaritan woman, even asking her for a favor. Unlike his countrymen, Jesus did not demean her for her repeated relationships with men, or for her Samaritan heritage, or for her gender. She in turn did not become defensive, but took responsibility for her life—exactly what we want our kids to do. Even when our children make poor choices, we can relate to them respectfully.

USING WEEKLY FAMILY TIMES WITH OBJECT LESSONS

Daily life pulls big withdrawals from your young teen's emotional and spiritual bank accounts. Weekly family times make deposits of purpose, strength, guidance, and wisdom. When the family meets on a regular basis, parents can consistently build in a positive account balance. You can use object lessons and brief discussions of a Scripture verse to make deposits that anchor a truth with an image. Approach these like a coach with a team, not a lecturer with a class. Have fun, share feelings, do something together, and, at the same time, have a small spiritual lesson.

I like to give parents hands-on experience in having a family time when I lead parenting workshops. One of my favorite activities is to take several odds and ends from my house in a big grocery bag to use for props. I purposely pick up things that I already have, without planning ahead, so that parents can see how simple this is to do. To start the activity, I break the parents up into groups of four to eight and give each group an object with the instructions: Use this as a metaphor and come up with several examples of what we can learn about our lives with God from this object.

Fathers and mothers at a recent workshop came up with these insights, all within a fifteen-minute period:

- Knife sharpener:

  - It has a specific function, just as we have a unique role to fulfill.

  - Proverbs says that "as iron sharpens iron, so one man sharpens another" (Proverbs 27:17). Why do we need sharp knives? We toss aside and do not use the dull ones. We need to sharpen ourselves and each other. (The discussion could then move to questions such as, How can we sharpen ourselves? How can we sharpen each other?)

- Brown baking potato:

  - It comes from the ground and is dirty until you clean it up. Then it is beautiful, but still has blemishes. Jesus cleans us up.

  - Its nutrition comes from the skin, which is often viewed as the undesirable part. Sometimes life looks like a bad situation on the outside, but we can grow the most from the difficult parts.

  - For the potato to grow, it must be connected to the vine, just as we have to stay connected to the vine, Jesus.

- Red apple:

  - If you slice it cross-wise, you get a star design, like the star of Bethlehem. Things come out differently according to how you slice them. Sometimes we need to look at things not as we usually do, but as God does.

- You have to let it ripen. Fruit development takes time and patience and so does the development of people.

DISCUSSING PROVERBS WITH YOUNG TEENS

Proverbs can be sprinkled throughout the week as needed for spiritual flavoring. Pick one to talk about at the dinner table. Use a soft, questioning approach to draw out your kids' thoughts about what the proverb is saying and how it might apply to real life today. Keep it light. Keep your own comments brief, to a sentence or two. You could ask: What do you think about this proverb? What does it mean? Do you agree? Disagree? Have you ever seen anyone do this? Here are some suggestions from the book of Proverbs (See Tips section for additional possibilities):

- Anger: "A fool gives full vent to anger, but the wise quietly holds it back" (29:11, NRSV).

- Pride: "A person's pride will bring humiliation, but one who is lowly in spirit will obtain honor" (29:23, NRSV).

- Speech: "Do you see someone who is hasty in speech? There is more hope for a fool than for anyone like that" (29:20, NRSV).

- Positive Focus: "A cheerful look brings joy to the heart, and good news gives health to the bones (15:30).

TO WHOM AND TO WHAT SHOULD WE EXPOSE OUR KIDS?

When our children were middle school age, we got together with two other families and rented the Genesis video series on Creation.

We gathered in one home, ordered pizza, and watched the videos over two nights. Everyone was encouraged to ask questions. The kids were exposed to other families with similar values, observed good scientific thinking and research on creation, and had fun in the process.

Expose your middle school kids to people such as Dave Hopkins, who, crippled with MS, quotes Christ from his motorized chair, "In this world you will have trouble. But take heart! I have overcome the world." Expose them to people such as J. P. Moreland, a Talbot Seminary professor, who writes about philosophical issues as they relate to Christianity and who confidently debates celebrated atheists and agnostics. To Joni Eareckson Tada through her tapes or books. To the music of BeBe and CeCe Winans. Visit a place such as the Holocaust Museum and discuss at home how to think about this tragic part of our history and what to learn from it. Talk about how such events relate to life at school this week.

TEACHING OURSELVES AND OUR YOUNG TEENS ABOUT LIVING ABOVE CIRCUMSTANCES

Read the entire serenity prayer at a family time and discuss what it means:[2]

God, grant me the serenity
To accept the things I cannot change,
The courage to change the things I can
And the wisdom to know the difference.
Living one day at a time, Enjoying one moment at a time;
Accepting hardship as a pathway to peace;
Taking, as Jesus did, This sinful world as it is,
Not as I would have it;
Trusting that You will make all things right
If I surrender to your will;
So that I may be reasonably happy in this life
And supremely happy with You forever in the next.
AMEN

A family must be built on spiritual values or it will drift away from its moorings as the tides rise and reverse. Changing culture tides that can erode family foundations are materialism, lookism (which Pipher describes as judging people on their appearance[3]), individualism, violence, and even an extreme emphasis on tolerance which eradicates values. It is God the Creator who anchors us in our tilting, rotating earth-world. Adherence to His family building code guarantees our family safety and security (on His terms, of course). When you are firmly attached to the most solid security base in the universe, what do you have to fear?

PRACTICE TIPS FOR SURVIVAL AND SUCCESS

1. Learn to discuss without defensiveness. Encourage participation with starters such as: *Tell me more. Tell me what you think. How did you come to that conclusion? Are you willing to look at other viewpoints?* When your seventh grader says, "Dad, I think your views on nuclear arms are from the medieval ages," you could first respond, "Tell me more what you're thinking."

2. Use yearly celebrations as times to refocus on your spiritual values.

   - Thanksgiving—We put three kernels of candy corn at each place setting as a reminder for all of us to share individually three things we are thankful for.

   - Christmas and Hanukkah—Focus on the real meaning of these holidays. Talk about the meaning of the symbols. Read the original accounts from the Bible.

   - Birthdays—Make an audio or video tape with a brief message to your young teen, speaking both about traits you admire in him and about the spiritual direction you hope for in his life. Each year, add on and replay it.

   - Easter/Passover—Have a Passover meal and service. Do the traditional symbolic cleansing of the house, searching for any yeast (symbolic for bad attitudes, for example) to sweep out as you focus on God's provision for human beings. This is a good time to talk about and forgive any old wounds and unhealed hurts.

3. Make it a priority to attend weekly services at your place of worship.

4. Plan daily prayer in your family's life.

5. Remember to include spiritually oriented music in the recordings you play. Ask your young teens which artists they prefer.

6. Create a "Lest We Forget" book, with prayer requests dated and then answers written in and dated. (This idea comes from Dr. Rick Langer, Pastor at Trinity Evangelical Church, and his wife, Shari.) As Kristopher said at age three, "Sometimes God answers 'Yes,' sometimes 'No,' and sometimes 'Wait a minute.'" Include lessons about life that you learn together and you never want to forget.

7. Try using these and other Proverbs for discussion:

   - Anger: "For as churning the milk produces butter, and as twisting the nose produces blood, so stirring up anger produces strife" (30:33).
     "Stone is heavy and sand a burden, but provocation by a fool is heavier than both" (27:3).
     "Anger is cruel and fury overwhelming, but who can stand before jealousy?" (27:4).

   - Speech: "A word aptly spoken is like apples of gold in settings of silver" (25:11).
     "Like clouds and wind without rain is one who boasts of a gift never given" (25:14, NRSV).
     "Through patience a ruler can be persuaded, and a gentle tongue can break a bone" (25:15).

"An honest answer is like a kiss on the lips" (24: 26).

"Do not gloat when your enemy falls; when he stumbles, do not let your heart rejoice" (24:17).

"He who answers before listening—that is his folly and his shame" (18:13).

- General proverbs: "Like somebody who takes a passing dog by the ears is one who meddles in the quarrel of another" (26:17, NRSV).

"Do you see persons wise in their own eyes? There is more hope for fools than for them" (26:12, NRSV).

"When arguing with fools, don't answer their foolish arguments, or you will become as foolish as they are" (26:4, NLT).

"A gentle answer turns away wrath, but a harsh word stirs up anger" (15:1).

"The tongue that brings healing is a tree of life, but a deceitful tongue crushes the spirit" (15:4).

"The generous prosper and are satisfied; those who refresh others will themselves be refreshed" (11:25, NLT).

8. Rent a video such as *The Hiding Place* about Corrie ten Boom. Watch it together and then discuss it. Here are two of her well-known quotes that inspire discussion:

- "Never be afraid to trust an unknown future to a known God."

- "Worry does not empty today of its sorrow. It empties today of its strength."

9. Use a Bible prepared for study such as the *Serendipity Bible,* an excellent resource.[4] The *Serendipity Bible* is designed to be used without any preparation ahead of time. Suppose you wanted to study Paul speaking in Athens (Acts 17:16-33) and have your kids understand how he was able to relate his faith to a crazy world. In this Bible, alongside the passage are three sections of

questions under the titles: *Open, Dig,* and *Reflect.* The first section begins with the questions, "If someone made a statue of you, what pose would be most appropriate? What inscription?" The Dig section begins with "To be noticed by these Greek philosophers, how extensive must Paul's activity have been?" The Reflect section starts out with "What distresses you spiritually about the area in which you live?"

In another example from the *Serendipity Bible,* 1 Samuel 17 on David and Goliath, the Open section starts with "How would you feel playing football, alone, against the Chicago Bears? Which direction would you run?" Dig begins, "What does Goliath's armor and weaponry reveal about him?" and Reflect asks, "What giants are drawn up against you in battle?"

You will find great treasures by studying the Bible and learning together with your middle schoolers.

7
SECRET #7:
PULL UP A CHAIR
ESTABLISH CONNECTION
THROUGH WARMTH AND
AFFECTION

Parents often complain, "I feel as though it just doesn't matter what I do. It's me against the world and I'm losing the battle." But this seventh secret is something you can do that will have results. In fact, if a family could only practice one of these eight secrets, extending warmth and affection would be the one to choose. A warm and supportive family is connected with their young teen, and that is the key buffer against substance abuse, suicide, and negative peer influence. Warmth and affection are like cushioning to the cocoon. They override negative moments. Acceptance, love, warmth, and nurturance say to your middle schooler: "You are lovable. You are competent. You are good." Young teens who have received this kind of warmth at home on a consistent basis expect to feel warmth from others and so develop better friendships.

Lindsey did not feel warmth and affectionate support from her parents. She never seemed to meet her parents' high expectations, and she felt helpless to talk to her parents about it. Lindsey struggled with depression and suicidal feelings. Her thoughts included: "No one cares about me. My life is awful. The world would be better off without me." When such ideas became the dominant life-rules of her day and she saw no hope for change, she began to think about suicide as her way of saying, "I quit."

Extreme hopelessness and suicidal feelings increase when the discouraged young teen does not feel as if the family is nurturing. Dr. Mubashir Farouky, psychiatrist at Loma Linda University Medical Center, explained why teenage suicide is a rare problem in his native country, Pakistan: "Families there are very bonded and often live quite close together." In that setting everyone knows that he belongs to a warm, loving family of several generations.

Researchers discovered that the amount of family warmth and affection influences whether a young teen uses alcohol or not.[1] When the relationship between the young teenager and the parents lacked this warmth and instead had signs of hostility and unresolved conflict, substance abuse increased. Without warmth, family stress is higher. Young teens from these colder, stressed homes said they felt resentful, embarrassed, fearful, lonely, depressed, and insecure. These typically unexpressed feelings act as withdrawals from emotional bank accounts and increase a young teen's vulnerability to substance abuse. Empty accounts seek deposits, even through the temporary soothing of drugs and early sexual contact.

WHAT DOES A CONNECTED FAMILY LOOK LIKE?

Some young teens describe their families as great with *connection*, the emotional bonding or the togetherness between family members. Families with students who performed well in school were compared with families of students who had academic troubles and had transferred to alternative schools. A sense of connection was the key distinguishing difference between the two types of families. Dr. Susan Mackey, director of clinical services at the Family Institute in Chicago, believes, "If these teens are not connected to their parents, they'll overconnect with their friends." If you hear your teen saying, "I would do anything for my friends," he may be overconnected. Overconnection with his peers means he may impulsively take his friends' changing values over yours. He may try marijuana, steal CDs, or even steal money from you to give a friend.

Overconnection also means he is needy and will continue to seek connection wherever he can find it.

So how can you develop the comfortable warmth of togetherness if you suspect your family does not feel the closeness you would like each member to feel? Talk together. Listen to your teen's perspective. Spend time just being with your teen in a nonintrusive way. Sometimes that means just sitting on the sofa with her, waiting until she is ready to talk. Smile more. Be friendly. Have family dinners and family times on a regular basis. Change your tone or style of communication if you are receiving reactive, withdrawn, or sullen responses. Set the atmosphere for a friendly and accepting discussion of needs. Warmth and connection in a family can be seen, felt, and heard.

Sandra expected to be supported and affirmed. Her friend Letisha had never seen a family like this. Sandra's mother hugged Sandra. Sometimes Letisha saw Sandra's mother hug her father. She once heard Sandra's father say to his daughter, "Honey, you must feel strongly about that." Supportive and affirming talks are the norm in connected families. Affection is comfortable and spontaneous, without being intrusive. Parents are able to validate their teenager's feelings and perceptions even if they do not agree with them. Robert, for example, can say to his stepdaughter Alissa, "It sounds like you're having a tough time with your teacher. Tell me about it." As one young teen wisely pointed out, "I think our problem is that we each have our own agenda, so I guess we have to listen to each other."

As parents, we show warmth when we are receptive to our kids' feelings. Our middle schoolers are experiencing rapid changes, from stellar leaps in their thinking as it changes from concrete to abstract, to puberty changes, to size and voice changes, to status changes. They cannot possibly know how to sort out all of their feelings by themselves.

A seventh grader's handwritten note to another seventh grader illustrates some of the confusion of changing priorities:

Julie,
Hi, right now I'm supposed to be doing an assignment for

Griffin but I don't know anything except that I could be skiing right now! With Jeremy! Why do I have to be sick? WHY!!!!!!!!!!!!!???????????????????!!!!!!!!!???????????!!!!!!

I WANT TO SKI!!! (WITH JEREMY!!!) (I'm yelling in writing.) I ♥ Jeremy (a lot) I ♥ Jason (a little) U ♥ John (a lot) U ♥ Thom (a little) U ♥ Bryan (a little) I want to go skiing! It would be so fun!! Except, I'd be embarassed, when I fell and my hair would be all messed up! Oh Well, I guess I'll have to live! I ♥ Jeremy 4-EVER! Jeremy said in a few weeks, he'd invite me again. Fun Huh?

Middle schoolers struggling with these changing opportunities need the security that comes from warmth and connection at home. Acceptance by peers is needed but harder to get. Connection and acceptance are so important that schoolwork comes in second place at best. All that middle schoolers used to count on as landmarks for finding their way in the world has changed in earthquake fashion. They can feel ten different emotions in the space of one hour and feel them more intensely than ever before. When parents give the message, In our family, it is okay to be sad, happy, angry, scared, loving, excited, lonely, or whatever we feel, they create an atmosphere of warmth and acceptance. The kids develop a high EQ (emotional intelligence). Research has shown that these families have kids who are able to develop good friendships and care enough about others to help them when they are in trouble.

REAPING

I learned growing up on the farm that if you want corn, you sow corn. If you want warmth and connection, you sow it by how you parent. Two types of parenting sow connection as they simultaneously guard self-esteem in girls, academic interest in boys, and peer popularity. The term *aware parenting* describes parents who are aware of kids' needs and of effective parenting approaches. Those parents who offer *supportive guidance* go a step further—they combine aware parenting with warmth. These parents use praise, show affection, offer help to their kids, permit their kids to do things, instruct them, and laugh with them. Their emphasis is proactive and positive.[2]

Such parents may offer praise that is direct, "You did a great job finishing your book report on time" or indirect (said to someone else in front of the teen), "Todd really helped me out today by folding the laundry. His stacks were so neat." Their positive instruction starts with an offer and respects the teen's time demands as well as their own, "Algebra can be tricky. I'll be glad to help you tonight when you're ready." They seek opportunities to permit their kids to do things: "Yes, I'll take you shopping for shoes tomorrow after school." "Sure, you can play basketball with Mike when you're finished eating."

Contrast this positive approach with a punitive parenting style. If you catch yourself doing these things—prohibiting, precautioning, ordering, belittling, threatening, and ignoring—you will need to make some changes. Even one-word negative responses are a problem over time. "But I hardly yell at him at all," you protest. Think about it this way: You may only threaten or ignore or prohibit him for 1 percent of the time he is with you. However, if each time takes ten seconds, that works out to seven such interactions every two hours, a very consistent reminder of how you are not happy with him.

Change your communication if you are saying things like: "You drive me crazy." "When will you ever learn?" "You're so sloppy with your homework." "I'll restrict you for six months if you talk back to me." "If you don't shape up, I won't give you your allowance." Repeated negative comments tell your teen, "You're not okay."

Again, parents have many ways to go about establishing a positive atmosphere of acceptance. Remaining open to your young teen's feelings and focusing your attention, you can make a measurable difference. Attention here refers not to giving material things, but to giving time and physical attention. Studies show that without focused attention from family members, middle school girls are not as popular and do not do as well academically. Middle school boys who do not receive focused attention tend to keep their feelings inside and struggle to be popular. When parents learn to give this attention, the young teens feel affirmed and important and develop their own voice.

Other research found that the support, acceptance, and closeness of fathers is especially important in order for middle schoolers to do well in school and to have healthy self-esteem. In this study, acceptance was defined as "giving quality time, not being too critical, being supportive rather than laying down dictums. . . . letting them see that you're putting forth more effort."[3]

Ashley, when asked what kinds of family activities had helped generate warmth and communication in their family, said,

> Sunday nights, family times during the year, before I got into cheerleading and Allison got into soccer, and Dad work, and Mom school. We read the Bible and discussed what was going on in each other's lives, and we'd go out to dinner a lot at Disneyland. [They lived minutes away.] We used to take family vacations to San Diego. That was really fun. We were away from all of our friends, not with people we know, so we could focus on our family.

Her younger sister added, "Vacations, away from our friends, and we can have fun with our family and that helps when we can have fun with our family, because then we can say, "That was a lot of fun. Why don't we do that again?"

Daniel talked about his family's activities:

> We all ate meals together. They [his parents] would ask, "What happened at school today?" We had to answer two things, two important things. We had a family council meeting Monday nights to coordinate schedules. At least we'd know what was going on.

A family without togetherness needs to make changes, yet keep their expectations low for what the changes initially will produce. It takes time to recreate a sense of togetherness and warmth. Changes can begin with an outside focus, such as playing a game together, watching a family-chosen video together, or working on a craft together, to develop the sense of comfort and acceptance that is the groundwork for connection. As time goes on, more personal concerns can be brought in for consideration. Announcing something like, "You really make me mad about the way you keep your bedroom floor knee-deep in clothes," is *not* a good way to open your efforts at togetherness.

Parents at a workshop contributed ideas of what had helped their families create an atmosphere of warmth, affection, and connection. Included were: camping and fishing, playing board games, riding major roller coasters, spending time with grandparents, building something together, and going on a mission trip together for the weekend. One family also said they created a Turkey Award to be given playfully when a family member has a goofy day.

MAINTAINING CONNECTION IN DIFFICULT CIRCUMSTANCES THROUGH LAUGHTER

When we were in Africa, a missionary explained to us that the most dangerous animal on the continent is also one of the tiniest. It is the mosquito, so dangerous because of the diseases it carries. Like the mosquito, a bad attitude in a family may appear to be harmless, but actually can be deadly. Laughter is a painless way to swat the bad-attitude mosquito and restore warmth. Proverbs 17:22 says that "a cheerful heart is good medicine, but a crushed spirit dries up the bones." Researchers tell us that laughter is a trait of exceptionally well-functioning families.[4]

Our own family has seen from experience the good medicine laughter provides. A call came from the hospital: "You'd better come down. Your daughter was in a bike accident, and she ran into a wall." I was alone that day, and I drove to the hospital to bring her home, thinking that a bike accident out with friends did not seem too serious. What the caller had not told me was that the bike was a friend's motorcycle, and the wall was a cement-block wall that was broken apart by the impact of Michèle's unhelmeted head crashing into it. Deeply bruised, bloodied, and swollen, with her clothes ripped in shreds, our daughter lay on the gurney alone in the emergency room.

Allowed to see Michèle for only a few moments, I felt frightened, sad, and a little angry at the circumstances which had brought her to this point. The nurse's ominous statement that she would now be wheeled off for a brain scan to better assess the damage only heightened the tension in the room as we realized the seriousness of what had happened. Michèle looked forlorn and dazed with her blood-matted hair, but then she observed quietly with a smile as she was pushed away, "I hope they find one there!" (meaning her brain, and we hoped so, too).

Smiles, then brief laughter began to replace the dread that had been building. The facts of the accident and of the damage done had not changed. Only our perspective had changed. Learning to laugh with your family, even at difficult moments, changes how you look at life and how you solve the problems inherent to life. As one writer titled his book, *The Situation Is Hopeless, but Not Serious.*[5]

That was not the last funny thing Michèle said during her hospital stay, which stretched into days. Her sense of humor did not keep the trauma surgeons from shaving parts of her long hair to stitch the wide gashes, but it did ease her and us as we watched her undergo the painful healing process. Months later as Michèle had scar revision work done, she elected to keep one two-inch scar on the side of her forehead, as a "reminder" of how much God loved her by letting her live. She later said she was thankful it happened; it forced her to see how loved she was and to re-evaluate decisions and direction for the future.

Laughing in the twenty-first century may be to families what jogging in the eighties and organic food in the nineties has been to individuals. Sometimes, as Matt Weinstein says, "The only thing you can do about your present life is laugh. Life is what it is, but you have a choice about how to handle it." Dr. Annette Goodheart teaches participants at Play and Humor in Healing Conferences how to laugh even when life seems out of control by saying: "Life is out of control, Tee-Hee!" You might try, "It doesn't matter what I do with my middle schooler; nothing helps, Tee Hee." Try it. It is really hard to say "Tee-Hee" without chuckling a little. The story of Norman Cousins, who literally laughed himself to health from a terminal illness, is well known. Think about it—being the parent of a young teenager is not even terminal! (Usually.)

Two vice-principals agreed on the importance of laughter in families with middle school kids. Judy Kissinger stated, "The most successful parents, I think, are the ones that maintain a sense of humor." Linda Kewin added her formula for success: "Maintain a sense of humor and just a little bit of distance between yourselves as parents and your children."

Humor and laughter can maintain warmth and connection while accomplishing tasks. Humor can bring two dissimilar ideas together. Roger von Oech asks in his book, *A Whack on the Side of the Head,* "What do John the Baptist and Winnie the Pooh have in common?" Answer: "They both have the same middle name."[6] Putting two unlikely partners together can unleash novel ideas about solving a difficult problem. What do a dollar bill, a glass jar, and bad language have to do with each other? Answer: An effective consequence for using inappropriate language can be donation of a dollar bill to the family charity fund in the glass jar, with the consequence the same for any offender, parent or child.

Parents often get into daily battles with their young teens over the messiness of their rooms, places which may house creaturelike clothes creeping out of drawers, down the dresser, and onto the floor. The daily battles rarely solve anything. When a parent, however, can detach from the serious struggle to prove orderliness is next to godliness, he often jumps miles ahead on the road to cooperation. As A. A. Milne said, "One of the advantages of being disorderly is that one is constantly making exciting discoveries."

Capture the moment. Cameras come in handy to record memorable moments to chuckle over afterwards. Keep an automatic-focus camera around to always be ready. (Even the disposable cameras take great pictures.) Our family still laughs every time we see two pictures quickly taken of Kristopher and several of his middle school friends doubled over (literally) in our family room, laughing after a little charade we pulled on them. Four of the boys were especially gifted in their abilities to hilariously and ridiculously insult each other (known here as *bagging on each other*). This particular afternoon, they were picking on each other's mothers, with outlandish descriptions. Rather than making any admonishing statement, we decided to be playful to make a point. Michèle ran upstairs and dialed a number to make our phone ring in the kitchen where I answered it in front of the boys with, "Oh, hello, Mrs. Carter [mother of the most talented bagger]. Yes, he's here." Dead silence reigned in the family room as I continued to tell her that, yes, they were indeed bagging on their mothers again. Although Kristopher had by this point guessed that this was a fake call, he kept quiet, and a horrified look spread across Clif Carter's face. Finally, unable to keep straight faces any longer, we laughed, and they all laughed, at both the craziness of it and the relief of the caller not being his mother. The boys did not bag on their mothers any more that day.

A little caution is needed with humor. Humor is not ridiculing or making fun of someone. Parents often make the mistake of teasing a young teen about some aspect of her appearance or about a new love interest and then wondering why they get such a sullen or irritated response. This is definitely not helpful humor. Neither is sarcasm, which can hurt with its underlying tone of unexpressed anger.

Humor helps you get a larger perspective on life. A sense of humor and a feeling of lightheartedness can bubble up naturally out of your thinking, your way of interpreting life. If you see life as a series of negative events and expect that the worst thing possible will frequently happen, you may have a difficult time improving your sense of humor.

To practice being lighthearted, buy a toy for yourself. My daughter bought a Koosh Ball for me to keep at my office to remind me that life is not always serious. (It even has an instruction manual, but I never needed it.) You might buy some clay and form a creature that reminds you of someone. Read a book of jokes. Once my husband brought home a book of jokes to read at dinner time together. The jokes were not clever or funny. They were, however, corny, and we laughed hilariously at the corniness of each one. He also has some rather unique and funny magic tricks. Share your favorite cartoons with each other. Post them on the refrigerator. Sometimes a cartoon can even express a point for you without triggering a reaction. Make an effort to understand your teen's style of humor if it is different from yours.

Whether through laughter, focused attention, listening, or affection, warm connection sets the atmosphere in a family for growth and cooperation and serves as a buffer against dangerous attractions. Overconnection that erases lines between people does the opposite; it stresses the parent and the teen and invites problems. Researchers report that young teens develop best when they feel close to family members and simultaneously feel free to explore and make decisions and mistakes as they build a strong sense of self.[7]

PRACTICE TIPS FOR SURVIVAL AND SUCCESS

1. Sometimes it is easier to see where more warmth is needed in your family when you list ways that family members feel controlled, parents included. Brainstorm with your kids—*I feel controlled when you* . . .

   - stomp out of the room.
   - scream at me.
   - lecture me.
   - never let me go to friends' homes.
   - ground me for two months without giving me a chance to explain.

   Instead, you and I could . . .

   - talk it through.
   - listen to each other.
   - pick a neutral place to talk.
   - set a time to calmly discuss things.
   - give more reasonable consequences.

2. Pay close attention to how you talk to your middle schooler.

Look for opportunities to say yes as you seek to support her in her life.

"Yes, I'll take you and your friends to the soccer game." "Yes, I'll be there to watch you cheer."

3. Look for opportunities to praise or compliment your teen, remembering that mentioning positives about him to someone else in front of him is valuable support as well.

4. Plan an hour or two without distractions just to listen to her, without correction or advice. Focus on understanding her.

5. Use humor and a sense of lightheartedness to increase warmth while dealing with problems such as these:

   ■ Problem #1: Name-calling and hurtful criticisms
     Solution: *Hand him/her the fish*—During a meal together or a family time with all members present, make a list of unacceptable comments, such as "That's dumb." "What a jerk!" "I hate you." "She's so stupid." "Duh." "Can't you ever get it right?" Then announce that whoever (including parents) forgets and uses these kinds of remarks will be awarded the "Fatally Inappropriate Slimy Hit" (FISH), a plastic fish you place on the table (adapted from Grace McOartland, who recommends this for executives). This is a little more fun if you find a rubbery, somewhat garish fish or even decorate your own. One reason this idea works so well is that it is lighthearted; it is easy to pass the fish to the deserving party without triggering a defensive response. You could expand this idea and come up with your own meanings for creature consequences: BUG for "bad and ugly groaner," TICK for "terminally inappropriate calloused kicker." Also try LIZARD or SPIDER.

   ■ Problem #2: Holding grudges and lingering resentments
     Solution: *Dump Your Garbage* (adapted from Grace McOartland): Have family members write down their

grudges and old resentments on three-by-five-inch index cards you give them. Talk briefly about how important forgiveness is, and read aloud, "Bear with each other and forgive whatever grievances you may have against one another" (Colossians 3:13). Do not read the cards or pass them around. Instead, have everyone tear them up and toss them into a garbage bag. Throw out the garbage bag. Later on in the week, everyone could be encouraged to talk about *how* they let go of grudges without mentioning what it was about. The person who does the best job or uses a creative approach to letting go of grudges could be awarded the Bear award (a small cuddly stuffed bear) for that week![8]

- Problem #3: One person dominating the conversation at meals
  Solution: *Flip a coin to see who will speak first.* You can also use a timer and set one- to three-minute limits. This takes you out of the controlling parent role and introduces a bit of levity into the time. One Christmas, Kristopher very seriously, but with a twinkle in his eye, gave his chatty sister a copy of the book entitled *How to Make Your Point in Thirty Seconds or Less.*

- Problem #4: Young teens who are furious with you, their parents
  Solution: Look at this problem from a different perspective. As parents, without the kids around, brainstorm and come up with outrageous ways to make your kids angry with you and with their lives in general. (These ideas are never to be actually used, of course.) One way might be to insist on going to school with them one day, then follow them to their classes and sit beside them, telling them how to sit, relate to their friends, and answer the teacher! Thinking of ways to make them angry can guide you paradoxically to see what their biggest needs are. This example would help you see how space, privacy, and a growing sense of control over their lives are important to them.[9]

6. Use some of these tips for adding humor and laughter:

- Buy a cartoon or funny calendar with one joke per day and keep it where everyone will see it.

- Make it a family project to learn how to juggle. Start by using colored scarves, which will float slowly up and down, and gradually switch to harder objects.

- Buy some jars of bubbles for the whole family and use them. Be sure you are not using them where any of your teen's friends would see!

- Learn and teach some simple magic tricks. This has been great fun for my husband, and we all laugh together.

- Watch a funny video together.

- Practice being lighthearted about your own weaknesses—like a tendency to be controlling. You can announce, "Here comes the schedule king."

8

SECRET #8: STEP BACK

ENCOURAGE AUTONOMY

Luann's dreams are a little unreachable for most people. In one of Greg Evans' comic strips, she tells her school counselor, "When I was little, I had really silly goals. I dreamed of being a ballerina or an Olympic skater." The counselor queried, "And now you're older?" Luann's response: "I want to marry Tom Cruise."[1]

Young teens, like adults, have both good and bad traits. Most of the time, they really want to please, and they can and will listen to you if you show them the respect they need. Even when their behavior shocks you, they have a deep need to have you believe in the person they are inside. Sometimes their ideas and dreams about life may seem ridiculous, but you can gain valuable insight into who they are as you listen with interest to them, consciously putting your criticisms aside. Rhythm and blues musician Tavie comments, "So many times parents have this mold already set that they want their kids to fit into. What I've done is expose my kids to a lot of things. That allowed them to find things they were interested in and then go towards that. Once I see that they're serious about it, then they'll get the support they need to make it happen."

Today, as I write this, I am reminded of Michèle, our twenty-three-year-old daughter (five-foot-three-and-one-half inches tall and petite), who came over to see us last night. When Michèle was in seventh grade, she began to talk about wanting to be a Police officer. Sometimes she would even say it was a dream of hers. We listened and occasionally tried to point out to her all of the dangers involved in such a job. She continued to talk about it off and on throughout high school, and we continued to try to talk her out of it. I begrudgingly went with her once to a meeting for police Explorers, teens who are trained and work with the officers. The time commitment was high and would interfere with school and her job, so this time it was easier to talk her out of it. We had other ideas for her. A four-year college for a start, then on to teaching or counseling (she would be great!) or even to the field of business, another interest of hers.

And so Michèle went off to college and began studying her way through. But the dream spawned in seventh grade never stopped growing. Sometime during the third quarter of her third year in college, after much reflection and investigation, she began again to discuss police work with us.

Last night she came over to show us her new uniforms and jackets with their red and blue emblems and their extra loops for a badge and a baton, clothes we bought for her entrance into the San Bernardino County Sheriffs Academy. Her dream from age twelve never stopped blossoming (although her dream at age five of being a Popsicle seller long ago dropped away). The question is, how could we of all people continue to put up roadblocks (she has already learned to jump them!) when weekly we hear clients in our offices who tell us they have always regretted following a mother's or a father's dream for them instead of their own. Michèle will probably finish college while on a police force somewhere (they encourage that), or she may not. My hope is that she will, but she is a very wise lady, and I know she will be able to figure out what is right for her. The proverb says, "Train a child in the way he should go," not in the way the mother and father insist that child should go (Proverbs 22:6).

Dreams born in the early teen years need to be respected, even if they seem totally wacky. They may or may not be good directions to pursue, but they can be respected and appreciated; they increase your child's sense of autonomy, and by knowing them you can better understand her heart.

Tavie further explained how he has paid attention to his kids' dreams and ideas:

> I took them places, like museums, and taught them a lot of history. When my son was in junior high school, I supported him when he wanted to try out sports. He played sports for a while and he did not really like it. I always saw him tinkering with electronics, so I bought him a computer, and now he is a computer wizard. I have friends that call him or come to the house to have him fix their computer systems.

Paying attention to your child's dreams helps him develop his inner self and his voice, the voice he must have in order to be able to say how he feels and what he thinks. Young middle schoolers get into much trouble when they disregard their own thinking, ignore their feelings and gut reactions, and respect themselves so little that they just go along with the crowd. It is not easy, however, to develop a voice when who you are is rapidly changing.[2]

Girls find themselves taller, filling out with curves, becoming more moody, and feeling new attractions to boys. A young teen girl is no longer anchored by the strong sense of self she felt as a child. She is vulnerable. Our culture blasts away at her. Her older sister tells her if she would just lose weight, she would probably get some boys interested. Her cousin says if she would just act dumb the boys would like her better. Changing to meet others' standards and expectations, she may give up herself in the process. *I think* becomes *What do you think? I feel* becomes *How do I look?*

A boy at this stage also needs to develop a sense of personal worth. His parents' attentiveness to what he thinks and feels, given without an attempt to show him where he is wrong, increases a young teen boy's capacity for independent thinking. He needs to be able to convince you, the parent who always had the solution, that his answer to a problem is just as good as yours and maybe better. Boys also need affirmation for who they are. This gets tricky, because as described before, they can easily minimize what you say if you use praise in the wrong way. To say, "You're so wonderful," can actually make him feel evaluated and judged. Even though it sounds positive, it can draw a negative internal response.

Praise to your middle school child has two parts: what you say and how he takes it. Direct your praise to your teen's abilities by complimenting specifics of what he does. "I like your book report. Reading it made me want to read the whole book." This praise allows him to reflect, "I did okay. I'm a good thinker, and I can explain myself." Another example: "Thanks for washing the truck. It looks new." His inner reflection may be, "I'm competent, and I can contribute." This indirect affirmation of who your child is as a person is often difficult for parents to grasp, but it is a crucial and effective approach. As your middle schooler feels affirmed by his family, he grows stronger as an autonomous person who can stand firmly on what he believes.

FOCUSING ON THE POSITIVES ON THE ROAD TO AUTONOMY

Chi Chi Rodriguez has often told of how much he learned from Smiley Blanton (fifty years his senior) as they played golf together, laughing and talking:

> He taught me that when I prepared to tee off, I must concentrate on the pin, not on the sand traps and water hazards in between. "Be positive," he told me. "Your body can do only what your brain sees, Chi Chi. If you think of the negatives, you'll be drawn to them. But if you keep your goal foremost in mind, you'll aim for it."[3]

What is the "pin" to concentrate on with your young teen? Her developing strong character, moving toward adult maturity, becoming a loving, giving spiritual person that you want to have a relationship with the rest of your life? Too much focus on the sand traps and water hazards between her and the pin can draw you closer to the problems and make her (and you) more likely to get trapped rather than see them for what they are—added challenge for the journey.

The sand traps and water hazards of the early teen years can certainly add some challenges to your family. A bad attitude, annoying noises (such as whistling), discipline problems at school, chores not being finished, messy rooms, poor grades, and "But I don't want to" answers provide a challenge for any parent. So, keep focused on the pin—respond to your teen as a person rather than react to him; worry more about your response to her than about her response to you; and remind yourself and your teen that this is indeed a journey and you will both get through this stage.

Understand that these "hazards" may be your teen's best attempt to deal with life. Guide, correct, and redirect him without shame and often with humor. When our son would trail me into a room where I wanted to work and would noisily "beat-box" (a unique method rappers of the eighties would use to set a beat/rhythm using their mouths and hands, tapping, blowing, keeping time) near me, sometimes I would say, "Thank you, Kristopher, for giving me *another* opportunity to practice *ignoring* you."

TAKING TIME TO LEARN THE MEANINGS OF THINGS

When we lived in France, we needed to know the meanings of things in French culture. Similarly, to really understand your young teen as an individual, you need to discover the meanings of phrases, expressions, and nicknames. As Humpty Dumpty once said, "Words don't mean; people mean." Understanding what the real person behind the middle school facade means is central to your relationship and to your teen's development at an autonomous, healthy individual. Keep in mind that the very things that stun you at first will later be the ones you find yourself smiling at.

A few weeks after the Gulf War ended, we decided to take advantage of the low airfare ticket prices to Europe. On the return trip home while lounging in the airport and wondering why our flight was late, we read in the newspaper and heard broadcast over the PA system that many of the airline workers were on *greve* (strike). Both Bill and I started laughing—it just seemed so *French*. Even though it was an inconvenience (when it happened the first time to us years before, we were frustrated with the French system), we thoroughly enjoyed the familiarity and nostalgic feel of the strike, which reminded us so much of our years in France. And we knew that sometime, somehow we would get home and that our anger or resentment would not speed the workers up at all. So we leaned back in our airport chairs and reminisced some more, reflecting on other warm memories that were created after we had learned to accept and even appreciate the French way of doing things. Hold onto the fact that you will be amused later by some of the difficulties you experience now with your middle schooler on his route to autonomy.

LEARNING WHAT GIRLS WISH THEIR PARENTS UNDERSTOOD ABOUT THEM AND VICE VERSA

At a workshop I gave recently for mothers and middle school daughters, I asked the daughters to list and discuss what they wished their parents understood about them at this stage of life. The following are some of the comments:

- I wish you would spend more time with me.

- I think I should be treated more responsibly and be taken seriously!

- You're overprotective and we want to make our own choices.

- I wish my Mom would understand that when I tell her something that it shouldn't be told to all of her friends.

- Appreciate what we do, not what we don't do.

- Sometimes I want to be left alone.

Mothers similarly were asked to list and discuss what they wished their daughters understood about being a mother:

- We're interested but we are not trying to butt in.

- (From two working single mothers) Put yourself in my place. We need each other. I can't do it all. I need you. You need me.

- Be a kid. Do not grow up sooo fast; you will have your chance.

- I think you are so wonderful. I wish you could see in you what I see.

- I'm not arguing with you. I just want to communicate or have a discussion.

Middle schoolers have their own way of seeing the world. Parents need to take heart because there can definitely be a time when it is possible to look back on all this, as we do on aspects of our experience in France, and smile. In fact, why not begin to enjoy it a little bit now?

FACING COMPLICATIONS ALONG THE WAY TO AUTONOMY

Since mothers and daughters and fathers and sons seem to come from different planets during these middle school years, crises will erupt periodically. To change these crises to mere complications along the road to autonomy, use some lessons learned by our friend Howard Ostendorff who was living in Africa when he encountered a different kind of crisis while whitewater rafting on the Tana River in Kenya.

Howard tumbled over a small waterfall that had been blocked from his view by an island in the river. The force of the river flow was so great that he lost his innertube, flipped backwards over his head, and was pulled beneath the surface. He panicked when he realized he was caught in a *hydraulic*, a vertical whirlpool that pulled him into its center. Gasping for air, he tried to swim downstream only to be sucked under. Exhaustion set in. The roar of the rapids muffled his cries.

As Howard reports,

> I was more scared for my life than I had ever been. I tried standing up and found a foothold for my right leg, my strongest leg. I braced to withstand the next rush of water, only to feel my leg give way as the inside ligaments were ripped and my leg collapsed.

Howard knew he was helpless and called on God for help, relaxing for the first time. He remembered the lifesaving rules: "Do not fight the current. You will get exhausted. Just get your breath when you can." The rafting guides had also said the day before, "Get on your back and trust your life preserver if you are thrown out of the raft." Howard got on his back, relaxed again, and tried going diagonally across the stream. Finally, the hydraulic released him, and he was rescued downstream.

Howard's sense of utter helplessness and abject terror could be compared to the intense panic parents can feel when they encounter the force of emotional rivers and hidden waterfalls on the way to helping their middle schoolers become autonomous. The following lessons from his experience can prepare you for navigating these trouble spots. Note: That does not mean eliminating them, just navigating them!

- Lesson #1: There *will* be waterfalls. Disturbing shocks and surprises will occur. From a *D* or an *F* on your straight-*A* student's report card, to a bag of marijuana appearing in your child's friend's pocket, to discovering your child has directions for making a pipe bomb—things will happen that are difficult to prepare for.

- Lesson #2: There *will* be islands blocking your view, so you cannot see all of the waterfalls up ahead. No one can accurately predict the specific problems that you will encounter. Parents never have total knowledge (that is part of

God's job), and the development of some problems can only be seen in hindsight, so berating yourself is never helpful.

■ Lesson #3: Your young teen is changing so rapidly that the force of dealing with her can knock you off your feet. A daughter who yesterday wanted a new stuffed animal may today clamor for a navel ring.

■ Lesson #4: Your usual parenting skills (your life preserver) may keep you afloat, but they alone may not save you. Sometimes you just have to hang on for dear life until you get to calmer waters.

■ Lesson #5: By using your natural strengths, you may actually weaken your position and encourage dependency, not autonomy, in your middle schooler. Our strengths in the workplace are often weaknesses at home. Walt's articulateness serves him well in his position as professor. At home, he may be seen as a lecturer who rarely listens. Sharon's position as vice-president of her company requires her to be aware of problems, to search for the person who caused the problem, and to figure out how to solve it. Using the same approach at home causes her young teen to resent her for her blame-focused manner. David's reputation as a lawyer is indisputable. At home, he seems to prepare a brief to defend his position, and rarely does a family member win an argument.

■ Lesson #6: Choosing not to fight the resistance (the current) may be your first step in the direction you want to go. A parent in a power struggle with a young teen may feel like a swimmer in a rip tide or a whirlpool, where fighting brings no success, only exhaustion. You can also picture the struggle as a tug of war, something that cannot continue if one person calmly drops the rope. When the situation is calm again, discussion can pick up safely.

- Lesson #7: Calming down inside enables you to be open to more possibilities. Relax. Get your breath. You can think more clearly and see a broader context that may hold a solution.

Martin Luther King's life was once saved by calmness and clear thinking. An attacker stabbed him in the chest next to the aorta. When a frantic rescuer tried to extricate the blade, King calmly asked him to leave it in. The emergency room surgeon later told him, "The tip of the knife was next to the aorta. If you had moved suddenly, you would have died instantly." Learning to be calm inside may not save your life, but it may save your relationship with your young teen when you hit a waterfall.

In the midst of a crisis, remaining as tranquil as possible, ask yourself, What is the truth in this situation and what is the truth about my middle schooler? Sally caught herself starting to panic when she found a disturbing letter in her daughter's room. She reminded herself,

> Sarah is thoughtful and careful. I have no indication that she is drinking. She has a faith and her own commitment to God. Just because her friend is bragging about drinking and not getting caught doesn't mean that Sarah is also drinking. I need to talk to her about this. I also need to tell her that I've been invasive and have read this letter. She will be angry with me, but I need to be honest with her. We can work this out.

- Lesson #8: Do not handle it alone. Look up to God and ask for His help. Make connections with supportive family and friends. As musician friend Tavie said about his family, "My grandmother was everybody's leaning post."

- Lesson #9: Try some new ideas (go sidestream instead of just the usual downstream and upstream). Neither grounding for six months nor, at the other extreme, saying "Boys will be boys" is an effective way to parent a thirteen-year-old just caught stealing. Enlisting him in volunteer work at a Salvation Army store would be a more responsible consequence. Let the solution come to you instead of trying to force it. Scripture gives some wonderful advice: "He who has been stealing must steal no longer, but must work, doing something useful with his own hands, that he may have something to share with those in need" (Ephesians 4:28).

Howard's drama reminds us that sometimes our best efforts using our natural strengths will not rescue us from the difficult entanglements of raising middle schoolers to become autonomous. The author of Ecclesiastes said it best:

Whoever digs a pit may fall into it;
whoever breaks through a wall may be bitten by a snake.
Whoever quarries stones may be injured by them;
whoever splits logs may be endangered by them.
Whoever raises young teenagers may be seriously demoralized
   by them.
(10:8-9)

(I confess—the original author did not write that last truism, but it is true!)

Perhaps learning to let go, to aim not toward mastering each crisis but toward responding with steadiness and serenity, compassion and confidence, is one of the most important gifts we can give our young teens. Allison expressed it well in her message to parents, "Calm down and try to take it calmly and the kids will feel more comfortable and feel, 'My parents aren't doubting I can do this.'"

PRACTICE TIPS FOR SURVIVAL AND SUCCESS

1. Draw a dream: Give each person a sheet of white paper. Use markers to draw the dream of what you would love to do with your life. This is not a time for criticism or judgment or even disapproval. Share and discuss the drawings.

2. Invite new thoughts and aspirations from each family member by picking ten to fifteen professions and having each person finish the sentence, If I were a _____, I'd _____. Examples:

- If I were a lawyer, I'd want to help physically challenged adults.

- If I were a doctor, I'd want to be a pediatrician and work with AIDS babies.

- If I were a teacher, I'd want to teach kindergarten kids.

3. Look for your young teen's unique strengths and point them out to her regularly. Examples:

- You really used your leadership skills well when you organized the snack bar.

- Calling Andy after his strike-out was a great way to show your friendship.

- I like the way you put your thoughts into words. That really showed your creativity.

- I notice that you seem very alive and happy when you play tennis.

- You show a lot of creativity in the clothes you put to-gether—your color choices seem so vibrant. (One father admired his daughter's creative choices after observing her grab a handful of colored socks, twirl them around in the air, and wear whichever two fell out first.)

- You made six assists in the game today. The way you cooperate with the team helps them all play better.

4. Try these ideas for inducing calm in times of stress:

- Remember that God's perspective may be radically different from yours. What may seem like a crisis to you may only be a complication—a complication that when resolved will produce something wonderful in the life of your teen.

- Count to twenty in Russian or French or Spanish or in any language other than your first language. Just concentrating a little more will help calm you down.

- Breathe deeply and slowly. Practice good self-talk—*This isn't the end of the world. What's positive about what is happening?*

- Learn to do relaxing things together. You might try flying a kite together or building a rock garden and small pond in the backyard as a place for reflection. At age thirteen, our son asked to build such a place since he noticed most of the families of his Vietnamese friends had one.

- Realize that sometimes creating a crisis is your teen's only way to get your attention. This is not an excuse, but it needs to be considered as a possibility.

- Read a psalm. Here are some sample verses:

  - Psalm 18:1-2, 28: "The Lord is my rock, my fortress, and my deliverer; my God is my rock in whom I take refuge. [The psalmist must have had teenagers, too.] He is my shield. . . . You, O Lord, keep my lamp burning; my God turns my darkness into light."

  - Psalm 27: "Though an army [of middle schoolers?] besiege me, my heart will not fear."

- Psalm 46: "God is our refuge and strength, an ever-present help in trouble."

■ Do family activities outdoors.

TIE IT ALL TOGETHER:
SUPPORTING MIDDLE SCHOOLERS IN THEIR SEARCH FOR IDENTITY

When I asked eighth grader Allison how she handles being around drugs, smoking, drinking, and other pressures, she replied, "I just say, 'I'm not going to do it.' That's just something I'm really firm on." Allison is on her way to developing a solid sense of identity. She is more concerned about who she is as a person than about what others think about her.

Dr. John Carter refers to identity when he describes what maturity looks like.[1] Maturity is having a realistic view of yourself and others, having values, being able to use your abilities, and being able to plan for the future as well as enjoy the present.

To develop a sense of self, a teen needs to go through the process of separation from his parents. Dr. Paul Lipkin says that "selfness begins with separation and it is the parents who must separate first from the child rather than the other way around." During the elementary school years, most children look to their parents and family for their source of identity. During adolescence, as they seek their own personal identity, they frequently question and react against the family identity. Author Simone De Beauvoir wrote that "identity is shaped only in revolt against someone." For an adolescent that means *you*, the parent! As one young teen said to me recently, "Secretly, my sister and I agree with a lot of what Dad says and believes in. But we've agreed to never let him know that, so we always argue with him."

This search for identity, especially in our time, involves pitfalls. Psychoanalyst Karen Horney said that because we feel alone and helpless in a hostile world, we create an ideal image to help us cope. But the ideal image is a fantasy, not an identity. Every time we compare our real self to our ideal self, we will fall short. Pipher writes that young teen girls seek this image by learning to be nice, not honest. Boys focus less on being nice and more on being macho. Neither is a direct approach to true identity. Choosing "nice" and "macho" over honesty creates a thin shell of a false self. Young teens with false selves go along with the crowd or cave in as life increases in complexity. However, identity based on honesty and values gives young teens a sure footing.

So how does self-esteem fit in with the whole idea of identity? Psychologist Mark Leary presented his theory recently at the annual American Psychological Association in New York. He proposed the idea that self-esteem is really just a gauge, like a fuel gauge on a car, to alert people to the growing emptiness of their interpersonal relationships. When self-esteem dips into a dangerously low zone, it is better to improve your relationships with others than to focus inward with affirmations of self.

Young teens are easily affected by parents' views of them. Since they are beating their wings against your cocoon of control, any interpretation from you may bring a defensive response. In their growing efforts to assume responsibility for their own thoughts and actions, they will benefit from parents who understand their need for friends and give them positive support, not critical interpretations.

One of the key contributors to self-esteem in a middle schooler is the amount of respect, acceptance, and focused concern that she receives from the important people in her life. When a parent makes daily deposits into the young teen's emotional tank and rarely communicates rejection or disrespect, the teen increases her sense of *okayness*. Feeling okay releases her to take risks and to develop dormant abilities, both of which contribute to her sense of identity.

Healthy self-esteem mixed with a strong sense of identity brings self-respect, which allows a positive response to criticism. Plunking down his hard-earned dollars for an unusual floppy hat he was buying from a Banana Republic Store, Kristopher smiled, then placed the hat on his head. In my mothering way I reminded him that it was a unique hat and that some kids at school might make fun of him for wearing it. "Then that's *their* problem," he replied without a moment's hesitation, and he walked out of the store.

MONITORING YOUR THOUGHTS ABOUT YOUR YOUNG TEEN

So how can parents facilitate this process of building self-esteem and establishing an identity? Since the family could be considered the matrix of identity, much can be done within the family to enhance this process. Our private, inner thoughts about our middle schoolers create the setting for this drama to unfold. How I think about my young teen will largely determine how I relate to her and how I may set her up to react to me. If I am thinking, *She's so flighty. She doesn't have a brain in her head*, I will deliberately look for her impulsive acts and overcontrol her behaviors. If, instead, I am thinking, *She has within her the ability to figure out the best choice of action, and can learn from her own mistakes*, I will give her progressive amounts of freedom and look for the occasions she is showing thoughtfulness in her actions.

As a parent, I always have a choice about how I view my teenager. When he slumps through the front door hiding his homework papers with a big *D* on them, what I tell myself privately will have a great deal to do with what happens next. If I tend to negatively distort things, I may say to myself, *When is he ever going to learn? Just like his cousin, he doesn't really care, and he won't try hard enough. I'll really have to clamp down now and ground him for two weeks*. This negative reasoning, based on fear and a tendency to jump to conclusions, will likely create distress, result in conflict, and leave the teen feeling that he is a failure or at least not good enough.

I can, however, respond to this same situation with more positive thinking: *He got a D. He must be very discouraged. He's usually so responsible. I'm sure he'll have an idea how to handle this.* Then I will feel calmer inside and be open to helping him solve this problem. My teenager, using the special kind of radar children have, will sense and hear that I perceive him as a middle schooler who can think and make changes. Monitoring my inner thoughts about him helps both of us be more effective and feel better about each other.

PICTURING THE YOUNG ADULT YOU HOPE SHE WILL BECOME

A sculptor has in mind what he wants to sculpt before he begins the lengthy process of chipping away pieces of marble. Michelangelo had an incredible ability to picture the end product of his work, so much so that it was sometimes said he was just releasing the figure from the chunk of stone. His *Prisoners* or *Slaves*, which appear to be half-finished sculptures, give dramatic images of struggling men emerging from the rough-hewn marble which held them captive. As parents, we should think like sculptors—when we have a clear picture of the traits we would like to see in our rough-hewn middle schoolers, we can more easily see portions of those traits emerge.

Simply noticing out loud what you see can reinforce those traits. As Ashley says, "It would be helpful if they [parents] would say like 'Good job' when you do it right. 'I've seen you try to change this.' They point out what you're doing wrong, but they never say, 'That was an incident where you've been doing a lot better.' It makes you feel good because when they tell you you're doing something right, it's easier to forget what you're doing wrong."

Look for ways that your young teen is exhibiting any of the values that are important to you and say so. To Justin, "I noticed that you're a really good friend to Cliff. Calling Sandy to ask her to help cheer him up was a thoughtful idea." To Jamie, "I like watching you play with your new puppy. The way you talk to him and train him seems gentle and patient." To Kyle, "I noticed that you started to get mad and go to your room. Then I saw you turn around and come back to say, 'Okay, Mom.' That was a great example of self control."

One of the most wasteful expenditures of energy is to continually tell a middle schooler *not* to do something. Neurolinguistic clinicians remind us that with this kind of instruction, a person must first think about what it is that you do not want her to do; then she can think about not doing it. In a strange way, through such communication you encourage your young teen to think about a behavior you do not want her to do. Telling middle schoolers repeatedly, "Don't be disrespectful to your teachers," may actually, to your dismay, increase their tendency to show disrespect towards their teachers.

Catching your teenager in the act of showing respect and giving him some positive reinforcement is a much more effective way to use your energy to accomplish your goals. Even noticing small positive steps in the direction of giving respect can be effective. Saying something as simple as, "I noticed that you waited for your teacher to finish what she was saying before you asked your question," draws attention to the positive behavior just exhibited without any focus on the negative.

LISTENING FOR CLUES TO YOUR MIDDLE SCHOOLER'S TALENTS

God has given your child certain talents and interests that may be similar to or radically different from yours. You may be as surprised as I was at the way your child's inclinations contrast to yours. I had always just assumed that our children would like math and find it easy as I did. My worst subject in school was history, so I knew I could be very understanding if they struggled with that. Michèle's worst subject was math, and her best subject was history. She can also just look at any electronic gadget, even the VCR, and fix it. The statement on the mug she gave me for my birthday expressed my contrasting abilities with gadgets: "If VCRs are so easy to use, how come I just taped SNOW WHITE MEETS THE SWAMP MONSTER FROM MARS!"

The melody of your young teen's life may not be what you

thought it would be. A melody is a simple core phrase or idea that repeats throughout a piece of music. Each child is born with a certain inner melody. Learn to listen for it and admire it as it reflects who he is. A life symphony built around that unique melody will hold together over time and be a blessing to others.

Michelangelo's melody was clearly artistic in nature. But, like many of us today, parents five hundred years ago did not always listen to or nurture the inner melody of their children. Michelangelo's father, Lodovico, saw art as manual labor and not suitable for his son. Lodovico and his brothers frequently beat Michelangelo because they detested art and felt that his interest in art was a disgrace to their family. Somehow Michelangelo persevered and for centuries has been revered as the world's greatest artist. If even the parent of an artistic genius can err in his guidance of his son, how much easier it is for those of us with normal children (whatever that means) to err in the training and guidance of ours.

ALLOWING TIME FOR IDENTITY BUILDING

Just as with financial investments, a parent's view with middle schoolers needs to be longitudinal; the current investments of time and patience may not show for years to come. As my friend Linda expressed it, "The thing I kept telling myself and I kept telling Michael [her husband] is that you have to have faith in the fact that you're putting out a good model, that the built-in traditions, the built-in celebrations, the built-in whatever sorts of things are one day going to pay off. It's a long slow process." Mature people take years to develop, with a lot of small (and big) investments of necessary nutrients.

Principal Otis says,

> I am a survivor of middle school [both in his personal life and as a principal]. Every parent has crises. One of the most important things is to just give the message to your children that you love them unequivocally. You don't have to like what they do, and you can say, "I don't care one bit for what you

did here; it's lousy, but it has no bearing on my love for you." And God will always provide you the opportunity to prove that, or two or ten opportunities. If we can convey that unequivocal love as parents through what we do and what we think and what we say, then we're going to get through middle school."

PRACTICE TIPS FOR SURVIVAL AND SUCCESS

1. Paper Bag Exercise:
   Assemble the following items in preparation for the activity: large brown paper grocery bags (one per person), magazines that can be cut up (a variety—fashion, sports, health), scissors, tape or a glue stick.

   On one side of the outside of the bag, write *Peers*. On the opposite side, write *Parents*. Inside the bag, write *Me*. Have everyone (including parents) cut out pictures and phrases representing these categories: (1) how my peers/friends see me; (2) how my parents see me; and (3) how I see myself. Tape or glue them to the appropriate sides. The pictures and words that fit the *how I see myself* category can be dropped inside the bag. Both parents and young teens pick examples that reflect how others see them today. Show and discuss the creations.

2. Have each person make a list: "Twenty things I would like to do in my lifetime." (This is different from the list suggested earlier for your family.) Read the lists to each other. No criticism allowed. Have each person choose one thing on the list that he could work towards now and then do so. Examples:

   - I want to sing a solo.
   - I want to give a speech in front of fifty people.
   - I want to visit Scotland.
   - I want to swim the five hundred meter race in five and a half minutes.
   - I want to graduate from college.
   - I want to visit Africa.

- I want to learn to speak Chinese.
- I want to own a wave runner.

3. Have each person pick out five to seven photos from your collection of family photographs. Tell what they show about individuals and about your family as a whole. Photos elicit stories and family stories can be grounding devices for flighty young teens. One twelve-year-old, Jonathan, picked a photo of himself getting a soccer trophy from his coach. "Mom took this picture because she was proud of me for hanging in there even when I didn't get to play very much. I guess teamwork and commitment are important to our family." Reviewing family photos in this positive atmosphere builds confidence and solidifies identity.

APPENDIX 1:
SUBSTANCE ABUSE

National drug experts tell us that the first line of defense is to educate your children about the actual effects of drugs. One police officer described drugs as the ultimate product, since once a teen is addicted, he will do anything to get the drug. This overview is not meant to be inclusive of all substances but gives information on some of the more common ones.

Alcohol: Sergeant Charlie Wilhite of the Riverside County Sheriff's Department has twelve years experience in law enforcement and is both a deputy sheriff and a lawyer. He also speaks to parents of middle school and high school students and serves as a Drug Recognition Expert Instructor for the federal government throughout the state of California.[1] According to Sergeant Wilhite, "The primary drug you will see in middle school is alcohol." A 1997 Indiana research project found the following statistics for alcohol in middle school:

- Lifetime alcohol use for seventh graders: 56 percent.

- Regarding binge drinking (drinking five or more servings on a single occasion at least once in the two weeks prior to survey)—

  - sixth graders, 7.6 percent

  - eighth graders, 18.9 percent.

Marijuana: According to Wilhite, genetic engineering and

cross-breeding have created a marijuana stronger today than the marijuana of the 1960s by ten to twenty times (up to 30 percent THC^2 content—the active ingredient in marijuana—compared to 1.5 to 3 percent). He explains, "To compare them is very difficult to do. It's like the difference between taking one aspirin and taking twenty aspirin. Intuitively you know that the twenty aspirin are going to do far more to you than the one would, and that's the situation we're in with marijuana."

Marijuana or cannabis (known as pot, weed, grass, hay, herb, seeds, whackytabacky, mary jane, twigs, maui-wowie, smoke, mo, and homegrown) appears to interfere with one's ability or willingness to pay attention. People under the influence have difficulty paying attention to two things at once, such as steering the car while also stopping at traffic lights. The drug also diminishes inhibitions and impairs perception of time and distance; it can disorient and may cause body tremors. Users will have difficulty staying in their lane while driving through curves.

The effects are usually felt within seconds of inhaling the smoke and reach a peak in ten to thirty minutes. Some effects remain for up to three to six hours after smoking. Because of the way that the body chemistry changes with smoking pot, the user may actually be impaired long after she thinks the impairment has ended. Urine tests can pick up traces of THC days after a person has smoked marijuana.

Long-term effects include lowered testosterone, chronic bronchitis, acute anxiety attacks, chronically low attention span, lung damage, paranoia, and dramatic personality changes in teens.

Inhalant Drugs: "One of the things that just scares me to death is inhalant drugs, like the aerosol gases, volatile solvents. Your average abuser of the inhalant drug, like polyurethane, glue, paint, is a male between the ages of ten and fifteen. . . . They're more deadly than cocaine or methamphetamine or any of the hard drugs you hear about," Wilhite reported. "An inhalant is basically anything that's in your home, any spray, bug spray, gasoline, and that's why they're the most abused drug for the ten-to-fifteen-year-old age range, because they're there, in every single house." Inhalants act as hallucinogens, putting users in a euphoric state, depriving the brain of oxygen. In the Texas survey, 20 percent of seventh and eighth graders reported using inhalants.

Inhalants are sniffed, snorted, and bagged (where the inhalant is sprayed into a bag to concentrate the fumes). The high may last fifteen to forty-five minutes, causing impaired judgment, breathing problems, nausea, vomiting, loss of self-control, and sometimes death. Long-term use can result in suffocation, brain damage, and liver damage. Inhalants used include correction fluid, model airplane glue, spray paint, hairspray, rubber cement, nail polish remover, and lighter fluid.

Certain signs indicate inhalant use—you will smell what they are sniffing; you may spot traces of paint color or pieces of glue on their faces; they may have spots or sores around the mouth and nose, red, glassy, watery eyes, a chemical odor on their breath, loss of appetite, excitability, and anxiety.

Other Hallucinogens: Wilhite sees an increase in LSD use in recent years. "Kids growing up in the seventies and eighties had heard horror stories of bad trips from the sixties, so they stayed away from LSD. The kids growing up today don't have that. They don't have the older brother or the cousin who went on a bad trip and hasn't been right ever since. It's a dangerous drug." LSD can produce good or bad trips. Often users face their worst fears during the trips. Senses are crossed, and users report smelling a color and tasting a sound.

Users of peyote will become sick within two minutes. They often believe they have entered the spiritual world and have visions.

Gypsum weed is a strong hallucinogen. It can be taken as a tea made of roots, or the dried-out seeds can be eaten on a pizza. It has been described as "pretty nasty, scary, rarely any good trips." Only kids who already think they live in a nightmare so they want something worse will use it repeatedly. Visual signs of usage include puffy areas on the hands; the skin looks like it is about ready to break out in hives.

Speed or *Methamphetamine:* While abused by middle schoolers, this synthetic drug is abused less frequently than the gateway drugs. (Gateway drugs are the more socially acceptable drugs that typically open the gate to harder drug use. Typical gateway drugs are cigarettes, alcohol, and marijuana.) Cocaine and methamphetamine are both central nervous system stimulants. "They act by speeding up all of the body processes; pulses go up, temperatures go up, users tend to be awake all the time and when they do go to sleep they sleep for a tremendous amount of time so their body can recuperate from the beating it has taken from the drugs. Speed or methamphetamine causes severe acne," Wilhite reports.

Speed's rush is quicker and lasts longer than powdered cocaine—less than one minute to hit and possibly lasting at a high for six to eight hours. Speed comes in three forms: rock form, powder form, and ice. Ice looks like light blue ice, costs four to five times as much as other forms, is potent, and is only smoked or shot up. The other forms can be smoked, snorted, shot up, and taken in capsule form under the tongue. Speed is not considered to be physically addicting but is psychologically addicting. *Speedballing* is using speed and heroin in the same syringe, which can be deadly.

Speed can come in various colors and is typically cut (diluted and mixed) with anything white: baby powder, aspirin, lactose, detergent, sometimes household chemicals such as cleansers and even Drano. A side effect of speed is that the body cannot process vitamin C and calcium, so the user's bones become more brittle.

Cocaine: The cocaine of today comes in two primary forms—regular/powder form and freebase/crack, which is more potent and dangerous. Both are physically and psychologically addicting. Crack cocaine is solid and is smoked. (In addition, there are approximately 155 types of designer forms created by changing a sequence in the molecular structure.) Be aware of these signs of usage:

- Change in appearance, which may include hair that is dry, ruddy skin, and not caring about appearance anymore.

- Becoming a night owl, avoiding the sun and heat, even becoming sick from heat.

- Having enlarged pupils, even eight to nine millimeters.

Heroin: This opium derivative is becoming popular with young white professionals again and has had some filter-down effect to teens. It can be a white powdered substance or something black and tarlike in appearance. For usage, water is added, and heroin is heated in a "cooker" (could be a spoon). A piece of cotton is used as a filter and the liquid is drawn up into a syringe to be injected. Tolerance quickly develops, requiring larger doses to get the same effect. Euphoria and relief from pain are felt for up to three to six hours for a new user. Withdrawal effects occur as the physical effects decrease, including chills, muscle aches, joint aches, nausea, and insomnia. Vomiting is frequent, and the stomach pain can be severe. Sweating and goose bumps, runny nose and eyes, and yawning may be frequent. Heroin is such a problem that TV and magazine ads are becoming commonplace to depict the awful side effects and withdrawal effects in hopes of discouraging usage.

RECOMMENDATIONS FROM SERGEANT WILHITE

- Know your kids. "The main thing that is going to tip off a parent to a child's use of drugs or any other problem is behavioral change. If your child has been the same child for the last twelve years, and now suddenly the child is changed, there's a reason, and, as a parent, you need to find out what that reason is. Maybe it's a problem at school, maybe it's something minor, maybe it's drug use. Suddenly wanting to sleep more, not wanting to go to school, hanging out with new friends or different friends, or not being interested in the same things that the child used to be interested in; those are all warning signs. You can't have drug abuse without some behavioral indicators." He explained how many parents see in retrospect the signs—an early riser now wanting to sleep all day, one who previously always made it early to bed now wanting to stay up all hours of the night, grades dropping from *A*s to *C*s and *D*s.

- "Be aware of unusual things—kids who don't smoke suddenly having lighters; kids having Visine [which he usually equates with marijuana use] in their backpack; kids carrying fifty tiny one-inch plastic baggies in their backpack; unexplained powders; some sort of a green dried vegetable stuff (kids don't walk around with oregano). If they're doing something they've never done before in their life, there's a reason."

RESEARCH RECOMMENDATIONS

- Educate your middle school kids about drugs. "Youths who believed substances were quite dangerous were less likely to actually use those substances," according to a Texas study.[3]

- Attend school events. "Students whose parents were involved were less likely to use alcohol and marijuana."

- Encourage your kids to get involved in extracurricular activities.

- Talk with your kids. Make sure they feel secure. The Texas study found a significant difference in the level of security felt at home, at school, and in the community by users.

- Have one parent or at least a very responsible adult at home with your middle school children after school. An Indiana research study revealed that most new drug use by middle schoolers occurs in late afternoons, from three to six o'clock.[4] The same study showed that if young teens reach the age of fifteen without using drugs, they are less likely to begin using.

APPENDIX 2:
STEPFAMILY STAGES OF ADJUSTMENT

When biological parents divorce and later marry other people, the new families have major changes ahead. The changes follow a stagelike pattern.[1] Knowing these stages does not prevent you from going through them. However, being able to label and understand what you are going through as well as knowing that there is an end to it may help speed up the process and help you deal with it with a lighter touch. Remember: Disillusionment and feelings of hopelessness are normal!

FIRST STAGES

The first three stages present an opportunity for the family to go forward or to stalemate. Going through stages one to three takes two to three years for an average family.

STAGE ONE—DREAM STAGE OR FANTASY STAGE

Both adults and teens have fantasies. The adult thinks, "If I just give him (the young teen) some time, he'll come to see me as his father. I'll just parent him like I did my son." The teen thinks, "If I just don't pay attention to him, this new guy will probably go away. He doesn't do anything the right way anyway." The biological parent thinks, "It's so wonderful to have a father for my son. Life will be so much easier now."

What is the task in this stage? To recognize the fantasy/dream for what it is, a wish that is not reality based.

STAGE TWO—THE REALITY RUB, WHERE FANTASIES CONFRONT REALITY

The spouses begin to grudgingly recognize that parents keep a strong bond to their biological children, in a way that seems to displace the new spouse. Remember, also, that every time this young teen makes a step of closeness towards you, she feels a strong stab of disloyalty to her biological parent.

Stepparents often feel rejected and lonely during this stage. Their hurt feelings and behavior can be seen by the biological parent as a desire to be out of the family. Patience is a necessity. Stepmothers in particular have difficulty finding a balance in their roles. Taking responsibility to discipline too soon produces conflict. Waiting too long erases the boundary between parent and child and thus decreases the child's security.

What is the task in this stage? To distinguish between the *shoulds* and the reality of the experience. To become educated about the normal stepfamily process. To face myths such as these created by typical stepfamily expectations:

- My prior marriage with its hassles is over.
- The way I handled my first family should work here.
- We should all quickly love each other.

The biological parent must support the stepparent in efforts to parent actively.

STAGE THREE—AWARENESS, WHEN FEELINGS AND MEANING BECOME CLEARER

Painful feelings are now recognized and accepted for what they are. The adults become more aware of what is happening and more clear on what they want.

What is the task now? For the couple to offer support and

understanding to each other as a first priority, recognizing that working on the marriage strengthens the security base for the children. For the family to allow and encourage grief to be expressed over the children's and adult's losses. Remember that grief is the God-designed way to deal with losses. Grief includes shock, anger, sadness, hopelessness, and anguish.

MIDDLE STAGES

This is a time of genuine restructuring. Average families take one to three years to go through stages four and five.

STAGE FOUR—EXPRESSING DIFFERENCES, TAKING A STAND

This can be a stage filled with relief as partners learn what the other needs. It can also be a stage filled with conflict as the family members struggle over whether the old family structures will stay or new inclusive ones will win out. One new blended family had a huge fight over one child's wish to set out cookies for Santa at Christmas. The struggles are important ones and can help move the family to a healthier system, loosening the structure from a rigid, frozen state.

What is the task? To hang in together as a family and talk out the differences. Help can be sought through your local Stepfamilies Chapter. Stepfamilies Chapters offer support as well as information about how stepfamilies work. Your local chapter can refer you to groups and therapists dealing with stepfamily issues.

STAGE FIVE—PARTNERING/JOINING TOGETHER

Spouses must express their desires and needs. The commitment must be strong to carry them through this difficult time. Some of the old habits and routines are usually kept, but with more flexibility, while new routines, rituals, and boundaries are also created. A strong boundary needs to form around the stepparent couple. As they cooperate on ways to communicate with the children, criticism of ex-spouses' styles must be nonexistent. The focus can be on what will be done in *this* family.

The task here? To regularly make decisions that help ease the pain and meet the needs of each person involved. Learn to listen and empathize. Create a family vision or mission statement, such as, "We are becoming a family of people growing spiritually and emotionally. We commit to regular family times together to relax, laugh, and talk with each other. We will find solutions that include us all. We are no longer the *X*s and the *Y*s living together, but the *XY*s, and we will incorporate many of both of our traditions as well as some new ones."

LAST STAGES

Stages six and seven involve consolidating the stepfamily as a unit.

STAGE SIX—ATTAINING SATISFYING CONNECTION AND INTIMACY

Parents and teens are now more open and comfortable talking about how difficult it has been to forge a new family system. An air of friendliness pervades their interactions. Stepparents feel more confident and solid in their roles, which include four features:

- Cooperation, not competition with the biological parent

- A clear generational boundary between the stepparent and the teen

- Approval of the spouse and the rest of the family for the role taken

- Integration of the unique qualities of this particular person, even some of the very things that the spouse and teens were angry about during the earlier stages

The task? To learn to discover and appreciate differences.

STAGE SEVEN—RESOLUTION AND DEPTH

During this stage, the relationships between stepparents and teens have become solid and comfortable enough that little thought is given to them—they just seem to flow more naturally. Interfamily crises and joint events such as weddings and funerals may still throw the family out of kilter for a while, but it takes little time to normalize again.

Stepparenting is always complicated. As you move through the above stages, you are also learning how to co-parent with an ex-spouse. Your child feels caught in a paradox as he loves two formerly married people who are now in conflict. Dr. Frank Leek[2] writes that a child can only respond maladaptively to this *Child Paradox*. Parents can release their child from this paradox by learning to "move from the intimacy/anger of divorce to the business of co-parenting." He recommends three types of communications to help this process: (1) Information calls, when parents call each other to exchange information on one issue in a nondefensive way; (2) Semi-yearly meetings to discuss and confirm scheduling for holidays and school activities; (3) Weekly telephone calls at an agreed upon time to keep current on items of cooperation such as counseling, clothing needs, and extracurricular activities.

APPENDIX 3:
ADOLESCENTS AND SUICIDE

Internal teenage risk factors include:

- a profound sense of hopelessness and inadequacy
- difficulty in adapting to change
- depression
- feelings of loneliness
- low self-esteem
- social isolation
- substance abuse
- stress that has accumulated over time
- feelings of being ignored by parents

Depression and hopelessness distort a teen's thoughts, affecting their willingness to make a choice as drastic as suicide.

External risk factors include:

- The death of a family member, a close friend, or even a much-loved pet

- Financial difficulties that are created by situations of economic insecurity, such as father's or mother's loss of a job

- Occurrence of suicide attempts by other family members, modeling suicide as a way to resolve problems

- Parental expectations that are too high, especially for younger adolescents

- Repeated moving of the home base

- Rigid and ineffective patterns of communication

- Breakup with boyfriend or girlfriend

Some suicidal adolescents reported multiple problems with their mothers. Stress between the two usually led to crises. They described power struggles and disagreements over what was important. When feelings were communicated, the relationship would become intense and highly charged with some kind of an outburst.

Some teenagers who attempt suicide may be trying to help the family avoid painful issues. One suicidal teenager came from a divorced family with both of his parents remarried. Although he hated the arrangement, he split his living time equally between the two homes, which meant giving up after-school activities and time with almost all of his friends. Frequently the two sets of parents would heatedly argue over the financial arrangements, and one parent would consistently show up late to deliver him to the other home. This young teen had decided that he was not worth the bother and that if he killed himself, there would not be any more conflict between the two warring sides.

A girl who was highly sensitive to the family level of conflict began to withdraw and spend more time in her room during eighth grade. The parents, who rarely talked together about family matters, thought that this was her way of breaking away from them, so they never pursued her. As she became more withdrawn, they stopped trying to reach out to her or show affection to her, thinking they were doing the right thing by giving her space. Inside, their daughter was in desperate need of affirmation and love, and her inner spirit began to shrivel. With it went her will to live until her first serious attempt at suicide shocked the family into action.

Some perfectionist children in rigid families are at risk. A rigid family is one unable to make changes to meet needs. When the unspoken family rule is understood as, "Smile and be happy; you must achieve and be competent at all times," the stress in a teen trying to keep the rule while knowing she is imperfect, incompetent, and unhappy can overwhelm her to the point of opting out of life.

The hopelessness, helplessness, and despair felt when a friend kills himself can also create a serious risk factor for a young teen.

Knowing the risk factors that contribute to a teen's suicidal thoughts and feelings can give us antidotes. The family with the withdrawn daughter, once they understood what she needed, gradually began to reverse their behaviors—reaching out noninvasively to her, greeting her warmly, asking her to join family activities. The parents started a process of learning how to resolve conflict between themselves without letting it spill over to contaminate the family atmosphere.

Cleaning up the toxins of the family with remarried divorced parents took more work. This teenager was actually caught between two warring factions. He was attached to both, but was torn apart inside by the stress of their war. He later expressed how much he wanted them all just to be civil with each other, courteous at the very least. These two remarried families had to learn that the cost of winning the competition between them could be the life of their son. Rather than compete, they learned to collaborate, respecting each other's limits, a very difficult task when years of animosity had damaged communication.

APPENDIX 4:
ADOLESCENTS INVOLVED IN SATANISM

Although most of the parents reading this book will never have to deal directly with a child involved in satanism, I have included this section for two reasons: (1) your teen may know someone involved or be affected by someone involved in satanism; and (2) reading about the extremes to which adolescents sometimes go can help you understand the deep needs your teen can have.

"I was a throwaway kid. Nobody wanted me, and I needed a place to belong. I had a lust for power, and I needed to find a place where my violence was acceptable." This was stated to researcher Clark by a teenager who practiced satanism.[1] Knowing what it is that propels a kid into such a bizarre attraction gives us clues as to the remedy, clues to the changes we ourselves may need to make.

"What has happened or not happened to a teenager that has promoted his seeking fulfillment from satanism?" Clark asks. As discussed in earlier chapters, teenagers need a sense of belonging, significance, and competence as they traverse the precarious path leading from childhood to adulthood. Limits and structure help contain the process. Power helps fuel the achievement of significance and competence. Curiosity and a need for novelty prevent boredom along the way. If the teen feels isolated, alienated, and detached from his family and peers, satanism offers the allure of fulfilling these needs along his path to adulthood. It even offers an arena to express anger and rage through revenge, which it promotes.

For your information, should any of your teen's friends become involved in satanism, the stages within the continuum of cult involvement are listed here.

- Stage one, dabbling or experimental use: This may start with a friend at a Halloween party. Often even this initial dabbling experience will seriously frighten the young teen.

- Stage two, social and recreational use: A fascination is deepening as the teen begins to study and learn magic, rituals, and ceremonies.

- Stage three, situational use: The teen has now begun to use satanism as a way to cope with difficult stresses in his life. He may even try to use spells on someone who has hurt him.

- Stage four, intensified use: At this point in the progression, a formalized initiation will have occurred. Clark described one initiation as "debaptizing" a boy who had earlier been baptized as a Christian. Teens involved to this degree will also become involved in thefts, drug abuse, burglary, and vandalism.

- Stage five, compulsive use: A high degree of secretiveness exists now. Rituals are more bizarre. Drinking blood may occur. The teen's psychosocial development will now be noticeably arrested or altered, meaning he will have stopped doing the normal teenage activities with normal friends—no football games, inline skating, complaining about parents, etc. Clark says that the prognosis is poor if treatment has not been initiated before this point.

- Stage six, chronic addiction: Satanism is now a way of life and very ingrained into her way of thinking and being. The teen may now be called upon to be involved in homicidal or suicidal behavior. The prognosis is poor for a full recovery at this point, although Clark states that she has seen it occur after a great deal of work.

Treatment is very difficult and lengthy at the last stages. It is far better to stop the process early and uncover the teen's unmet needs, finding appropriate ways to meet them within the family. Better yet is to understand with empathy the young teen's needs before they risk going unmet.

APPENDIX 5:
ADOLESCENTS AND EATING DISORDERS

Eating disorders came close to us when one of our children had a friend whose weight dropped to sixty-nine pounds. Young teens with such problems may die as their weight dips precariously low, and those who live may suffer organ damage. Eating disorders are serious and can be life threatening.

The dynamics for the creation of an eating disorder can be set up during the early teen years, since it is so easy to get hooked into power struggles with this age group. Some parents overreact to a daughter's weight gain or loss by trying to take control of her eating habits. If the daughter feels powerless against her parents in other areas of her life, she may resist their efforts and devlop eating patterns that become rigid and unhealthy. The body shape changes of the middle school years invite problems, especially for girls. As Mary Pipher writes, "To be a woman is to have a body image problem."[1]

An eating disorder develops as a way to cope with a problem. It has to do with the young teen's attempt to gain control over her life and to compensate for her need for bonding and acceptance.

ANOREXIA NERVOSA

Anorexia is a pattern of ignoring the body's natural hunger signals. It can start with a decision to lose a few pounds. If the diet patterns become rigid, anorexia can develop. It usually includes compulsive exercise. As the body weight drops, menstrual periods cease, and the anorexic's thinking becomes progressively distorted. She will see herself as fat and worthless. Her self-criticism escalates as her depression increases. In the latter stages with profound weight loss, medical treatment and hospitalization are often necessary. Group and family therapy will be needed as well.

Possible danger signals include:

■ constant checking of weight

■ a major unhealthy increase in athletic activities

■ an obsession with food and calories

■ a persistent tendency to toy with food

■ a penchant for cutting food into tiny pieces

■ following rigid rituals regarding eating behaviors, such as always eating from one particular plate

Since power struggles never work with young teenagers, seek to empower your child instead. The goal is to have her take charge of this problem. You can encourage that by:

■ Expressing your concern in *I statements* that say what you have observed and your concern. This keeps you from being critical and judgmental, which is counterproductive.

■ Giving up trying to control your child's behaviors and admitting your own helplessness over her ultimate choices.

■ Setting limits on what you will and will not accept. For example, boycotting family dinners is not okay. Neither is family criticism of your child's choices.

■ Seeking to understand and accept her feelings rather than trying to talk her out of them. Use comments such as, "You said you're feeling unloved. Tell me about it."

BULIMIA

Bulimia is a pattern of cyclical binge eating followed with purging by vomiting, using laxatives, or using diuretics, and it is accompanied by depressive thoughts. It could be described as acting on a food addiction followed by attempts to undo what was just done. Eating large quantities of food is a way to ignore or numb feelings. Young teens who struggle with bulimia seldom express their anger well. Triggers for bulimia can be sudden rejection, ongoing anger that has been ignored, and sometimes a childhood trauma, even sexual abuse, that has been minimized or never discussed. Bulimia, like anorexia, is a way to cope and an attempt to communicate an unspoken problem. Medical help and therapy may be needed.

Here are some suggestions for the parent:

- Express your concern by saying something like, "I heard you vomiting in the bathroom late last night. I'm worried." Then pause, respect the silence, wait for a response. Lectures never help.

- Since you cannot control her behavior, seek to understand her feelings and the underlying problems.

- Set limits on what you will and will not accept. For example, stealing food or money to buy food is not okay. It is okay to say, "I feel angry when . . . " whether you are the parent or the young teen.

- Since most young teens with bulimia have problems with boundaries, it is important to model strong flexible boundaries as well as to respect her boundaries. This means taking responsibility for how *you* relate to her. Treat her as someone who has the capability to manage her eating. That means you as the parent don't try to take over her eating habits. This helps the teen to establish better boundaries with others.

OBESITY

Obesity is a devastating problem for middle school boys and girls who are 20 percent heavier than normal for their build. The importance our culture places on looks has escalated in recent years. Kids' healthy defenses are not fully developed until they are older, and the teasing from others can overwhelm their fragile egos. Obesity frequently develops as an attempt to fill the heart through the stomach. Obesity insulates and isolates the young teen from the peers he so desperately needs. (I am differentiating between large and obese. Some children are naturally large and healthfully so. Parents need to help these kids fully accept their God-given body shapes and focus on being healthy.)

As the parent, you can help a middle schooler who is obese in the ways he most needs it:

- Use opportunities to express your love and concern nonverbally as well as verbally. A hug, a touch on the arm, and eye contact all help to fill the empty emotional tank.

- Focus on healthy eating, not deprivation. Starting a dieting cycle can set up a lifelong problem with eating.

- Seek to accept, understand, and elicit what the teen would like to do about the problem.

- Differentiate self-esteem and self-acceptance from appearance. Check what you model in this regard.

- Help your middle schooler to be assertive and express what he thinks, feels, and wants.

- Do further reading.[2]

NOTES

THE COLLISION: FAMILY, CULTURE, AND THE YOUNG TEEN

1. Frank Pittman, *Turning Points: Treating Families in Transition and Crisis* (New York: Norton, 1987) 175.

2. Mary Pipher, *Reviving Ophelia: Saving the Selves of Adolescent Girls* (New York: Ballantine, 1994) 12.

3. The "36 month window of vulnerability" was documented by research done by the Indiana Prevention Resource Center (IPRC) at Indiana University in 1997. Data was collected from 255 schools from 82 communities yielding 72,571 usable surveys from grades 6-11. For more complete documentation, see website: http://www.drugs.indiana.edu/drug_stats/intro97.html

Similar drug research has emerged from other states as well. See the Texas School Survey of Substance Use Among Students at website: http://www.tcada. state.tx.us/research/grades 7-12/execsumm.html

4. Baltimore city schools report the median age of first sexual intercourse to be 13 for girls and 12 for boys. Researchers at Johns Hopkins School of Medicine discovered 18% of the sexually active middle schoolers at Baltimore's Harlem Park School to have chlamydia. (Susan Okie, "Teenage Chlamydia Cases Alarm Experts," *Los Angeles Times* 3 Sept. 1997: E2.)

5. A. Miller, *Banished Knowledge: Facing Childhood Injuries* (New York: Doubleday, 1988) 5.

6. Several studies support the statement that the family remains the primary influence on young teenagers: Resnick's study published in *JAMA* in 1997 surveyed 12,118 teens from grades 7 through 12, giving separate statistics for middle school and high school. The study indicated that connection to the family as well as connection with the school is critical to the child's adjustment and protection against risky behaviors. (M. D. Resnick et al., "Protecting Adolescents from Harm," *JAMA* 278.10 [1997]: 823-865.) Some of the other studies supporting this view include Kafka and London, Foxcroft and Lowe, Field, Lang, Yando, and Bendell, Denton and Kampfe, Brown and Mann, Beman, Anderson and Henry, Adams, Overholser, and Lehnert.

7. Deborah Tannen, *You Just Don't Understand* (New York: Ballantine, 1990) 280-282.

SECRET #1: OPEN THE DOOR

1. Greg Evans, "Luann," cartoon, *Los Angeles Times* 1987.

2. Erikson, cited in P. H. Miller, *Theories of Developmental Psychology* (San Francisco: Freeman, 1983) 165-170.

3. J. Siegel and M. F. Shaughnessy, "There's a First Time for Everything: Understanding Adolescence," *Adolescence* 30.117 (1995): 217.

4. Siegel and Shaughnessy 217.

5. Resnick et al. 828.

6. Maya Angelou, *I Know Why the Caged Bird Sings* (New York: Bantam, 1969) 201.

7. W. R. Beavers, *Successful Marriage: A Family Systems Approach to Couples Therapy* (New York: Norton, 1985) 224-225.

8. J. M. Perry, R. W. Griggs, and R. Griggs, *The Road to Optimism* (San Ramon: Manfit Press, 1996).

SECRET #2: WALK CAREFULLY

1. K. Issler and R. Habermas, *How We Learn: A Christian Teacher's Guide to Educational Psychology* (Grand Rapids: Baker, 1994) 81.

2. Linda Ellerbee, "Quitting Smoking Helps, but the After-Effects May Linger Forever," *San Bernadino Sun* 4 Feb. 1995: A7.

3. "Psychological myopia" was coined as a term by Brooks-Gunn and Zahaykevich and discussed further by Paul Trad in his article, "Adolescent Girls and Their Mothers: Realigning the Relationship," *The American Journal of Family Therapy* 23.1 (1995): 9-24.

4. Family togetherness concepts and beliefs in healthy family systems are adapted from W. R. Beavers, *Psychotherapy and Growth: A Family Systems Perspective* (New York: Brunner/Mazel, 1977).

5. D. Baumrind, "Effective Parenting During the Early Adolescent Transition," *Advances in Family Research. Vol. 2, Family Transitions,* ed. P. A. Cowan and E. M. Hetherington (Hillsdale: Erlbaum, 1991) 111-163. For further discussion of the four parenting styles, see Maccoby and Martin, "Socialization in the Context of the Family: Parent-Child Interation," *Handbook of Child Psychology,* ed. P. H. Mussen and E. M. Hetherington (New York: Wiley, 1983).

6. For a discussion of "coercion, love withdrawal, and induction," see Anderson and Henry, "Family System Characteristics and Parental Behaviors as Predictors of Adolescent Substance Use," *Adolescence* 29.114 (1994): 405-420.

7. P. Bronstein et al., "Family and Parenting Behaviors Predicting Middle School Adjustment: A Longitudinal Study," *Family Relations* 45 (1996): 416.

8. H. G. Ginott, *Between Parent and Teenager* (New York: Avon, 1969) 41.

9. J. Gottman, *Why Marriages Succeed or Fail* (New York: Simon and Schuster, 1994) 116-117.

10. J. Gottman, *The Heart of Parenting: Raising an Emotionally Intelligent Child* (New York: Simon and Schuster, 1994) 17, 25.

SECRET #3: ALWAYS KNOCK FIRST

1. Mary Pipher, *The Shelter of Each Other: Rebuilding Our Families* (New York: Grosset/Putnam Book, 1996) 86.

2. Henry Cloud, *When Your World Makes No Sense* (Nashville: Nelson, 1990) 105.

3. This idea was demonstrated in a study of alcoholic families with boys identified as "likely to get in trouble," ages 10 to 16. These boys were followed up and interviewed later when they were 45 to 53. Of the boys in families where the mother had a high regard for her alcoholic husband, almost twice as many became alcoholics themselves as did the boys with mothers who did not have high esteem for the alcoholic fathers. If the one who drinks excessively is the powerful one, his behaviors are more likely to be emulated. When these young teens grew older and felt powerless, drinking was the solution they had learned. The modeling in these cases was not only the father's drinking but also the mother's attitude towards his drinking (A. D. Ullman and A. Orenstein, "Why Some Children of Alcoholics Become Alcoholics: Emulation of the Drinker," *Adolescence* 29.113 [1994]: 1-11).

4. B. K. Barber and C. Buehler, "Family Cohesion and Enmeshment: Different Constructs, Different Effects," *Journal of Marriage and Family* 58 (1996): 433-441.

5. Trespassing across your teen's boundaries invariably produces a strong emotional reaction and/or behavior. Suicidal behavior can sometimes be seen as that strong response to the trespass. A suicide attempt then could be seen as a screaming signal to the parents that the boundaries aren't right and that more appropriate parental supervision and nurturance and also, paradoxically, autonomy from the parents (evidence of good boundaries) are needed. Keep in mind that autonomy doesn't equal alienation. The two are actually opposites. Koopmans's research suggests that suicide may be a response to boundary trespasses (M. Koopmans, "A Case of Family Dysfunction and Teenage Suicide Attempt: Applicability of a Family Systems Paradigm," *Adolescence* 30.117 [1995]: 87-94).

6. *The Gospel According to Matthew* (3-part video series), The Visual Bible International, distributed by Gener8Xion Entertainment, Inc., P.O. Box 6548-347, Orange, CA 92613.

7. Issler and Habermas 56.

8. Issler and Habermas 55.

9. The study of 585 adolescents researching the concept of inclusion in family decision making came from the research by J. C. Brown and L. Mann, "The Relationship Between Family Structure and Process Variables and Adolescent Decision Making," *Journal of Adolescence* 13 (1990): 25-37.

SECRET #4: TURN DOWN THE HEAT

1. Walt Kempler, *Principles of Gestalt Family Therapy* (Costa Mesa: The Kempler Institute, 1974) 68.

2. Research shows that when angry confrontations between parent and young teen are frequent, a teen's emotional adjustment is poor (A. Tesser, "Conflict, the Role of Calm and Angry Parent-Child Discussion in Adolescent Adjustment," *Journal of Social and Clinical Psychology* 8.3 [1989]: 317-330).

3. A. Allentuck, "Thriving on Service," *The Price Costco Connection* 10.2 (1995): 11.

4. T. Szulc, "How to Talk to a Dictator," *Parade Magazine* 14 Sept. 1997: 6-8.

5. K. Blanchard and S. Johnson, *The One Minute Manager* (New York: Morrow, 1982) 39.

6. Gottman, *Why Marriages Succeed.*

7. The elements of an apology discussion is based to some degree on the work of Aaron Lazare, "Go Ahead Say You're Sorry," *Psychology Today* Jan.-Feb. 1995: 40-78.

8. D. B. Wexler, *The Prism Workbook: A Program for Innovative Self-Management* (New York: Norton, 1991) 48-49.

9. Lazare 43.

SECRET #5: SHARE POWER

1. Ginott 55.

2. D. Goleman, *Emotional Intelligence* (New York: Bantam, 1995) 190-194.

3. J. Middleton-Moz, *Children of Trauma* (Deerfield Beach: Health Communications, 1989) 13, 15.

SECRET #6: MATCH YOUR WALK AND YOUR TALK

1. Resnick et al.

2. The origin of the Serenity Prayer is unknown. It may date as far back as the philosopher Boethius (A.D. 500). The prayer is often attributed to Reinhold Niebuhr, but he credited Friedrich Oetinger, an eighteenth-century theologian. In 1947, Niebuhr read the prayer in an obituary in the New York *Tribune*. He liked it so much, he shared it with Bill W. of Alcoholics Anonymous. Because it seemed so fitting for AA, it has since been associated with that group.

3. Mary Pipher, *Hunger Pains: The Modern Woman's Tragic Quest for Thinness* (New York: Ballantine, 1995) 16.

4. Lyman Coleman et al., ed., *The NIV Serendipity Bible: 10th Anniversary Edition* (Grand Rapids: Zondervan, 1996).

SECRET #7: PULL UP A CHAIR

1. Resnick et al. 829.

2. Bronstein et al. 420.

3. Research findings on fathers' acceptance comes from Rex Forehand, as reported by B. Hendrick. Forehand found that even in divorced families, the father's acceptance was key to the child feeling a strong sense of self-worth

(B. Hendrick, "Supportive Dads are a Key to Success," *San Bernadino Sun* 13 Nov. 1994).

4. Bronstein et al.

5. P. Watzlawick, *The Situation Is Hopeless, But Not Serious* (New York: Norton, 1983).

6. R. von Oech, *A Whack on the Side of the Head: How You Can Be More Creative* (New York: Warner Books, 1990).

7. Barber and Buehler.

8. Adapted from Grace McOartland, "Betterways," *Bottom Line* 15 Aug. 1994.

9. Adapted from Grace McOartland.

SECRET #8: STEP BACK

1. Greg Evans, "Luann," cartoon, *Los Angeles Times* 22 Feb. 1989: V5.

2. Reiss conducted research on families and found that young teens developed their own voice better when they were allowed to convince parents that their ideas had merit and sometimes were even better than their parents' ideas. (D. Reiss and D. Klein, "Paradigms and Pathogenesis: A Family-Centered Approach to Problems of Etiology and Treatment of Psychiatric Disorders," *Family Interaction and Psychopathology: Theories, Methods, and Findings*, ed. T. Jacob [New York: Plenum, 1987] 203-255.)

3. Chi Chi Rodriguez, "Linking Golfers Around the World in Christ," *Links Letter* 8.5 (1988): 1-6.

TIE IT ALL TOGETHER: SUPPORTING MIDDLE SCHOOLERS IN THEIR SEARCH FOR IDENTITY

1. John Carter, "Maturity: Psychological and Biblical," *Journal of Psychology and Theology* 5 (1974): 183.

APPENDIX 1: SUBSTANCE ABUSE

1. Other drug information comes from a Drug Recognition Seminar given at Loma Linda University Behavioral Medicine Center by Detective Steve Dickey of Redlands, California Police Department, and from *Drug Identification and Symptom Manual* published by National Consumer Publications, Inc., 1994 edition.

2. THC stands for Delta-9 Tetrahydrocannabinol. THC is mainly found in the leaves and flowers of the plant.

3. Texas Commission on Alcohol and Drug Abuse [TCADA] 1997 study on grades 7-12. Website: www.tcada.state.tx/research.html or TCADA, Library/Clearinghouse Department/9001 North IH-35, Suite 105, Austin, TX 78753-5233, phone: (512) 349-6646.

4. Indiana University, The Indiana Prevention Resource Center (IPRC) Survey, 1997. Website: www.drugs.indiana.edu/drugs_stats/intro97.html

APPENDIX 2: STEPFAMILY STAGES OF ADJUSTMENT

1. The following information on stages has been adapted from P. L. Papernow ("The Stepfamily Cycle: An Experiential Model of Stepfamily Development," *Family Relations* July 1984: 355-363. Available: 1910 West County Road B, Suite 147, St. Paul, MN 55113) and P. K. Gerlach, *Stepfamily in Formation* (1997). Available: SAI, Inc. P.O. Box 3124, Oak Park, IL 60303. *Stepfamilies Stepping Ahead, an Eight Step Program for Successful Family Living* is also a good resource. (Mala Burt, ed. [Lincoln: Stepfamilies Press, 1989]. Available: [402] 477-7838.)

2. Dr. Frank Leek can be reached at P.O. Box 2468, Fair Oaks, CA 95628.

APPENDIX 4: ADOLESCENTS INVOLVED IN SATANISM

1. C. M. Clark, "Clinical Assessment of Adolescents Involved in Satanism," *Adolescence* 29.114 (1994): 461.

APPENDIX 5: ADOLESCENTS AND EATING DISORDERS

1. Pipher, *Hunger Pains* 4.

2. Resources include:

Greg Jantz, *Hope, Help, and Healing for Eating Disorders* (Wheaton: Harold Shaw, 1995).

B. McFarland and T. Baker-Baumann, *Feeding the Empty Heart* (Center City: Hazelden, 1988).

Frank Minirth and Paul Meier, *Love Hunger: Recovery from Food Addiction* (Nashville: Thomas Nelson, 1990).

J. Mitchell, *Anorexia* (Center City: Hazelden, 1985).

American Anorexia/Bulimia Association, Inc. 165 West 46th Street, #1108, New York, NY 10036. (212) 575-6200 Website: http://www.members.aol.com/amanbu/fandf.html

Eating Disorders Awareness and Prevention, Inc. (EDAP) 603 Stewart Street, Suite 803, Seattle, WA 98101. (206) 382-3587 Website: http://www.members.aol.com/edapinc

BIBLIOGRAPHY

Adams, D. M., J. C. Overholser, and K. L. Lehnert. "Perceived Family Functioning and Adolescent Suicidal Behavior." *Journal of American Academy of Child and Adolescent Psychiatry* 33.4 (1994): 498-507.

Allentuck, A. "Thriving on Service." *The Price Costco Connection* 10.2 (1995): 1-11.

Anderson, F. A., and C. S. Henry. "Family System Characteristics and Parental Behaviors as Predictors of Adolescent Substance Use." *Adolescence* 29.114 (1994): 405-420.

Angelou, M. *I Know Why the Caged Bird Sings.* New York: Bantam, 1969.

Augsburger, D. *Caring Enough to Hear and Be Heard.* Ventura: Regal Books, 1982.

"At Last—A Rejection Detector!" *Psychology Today* Nov.-Dec. 1995: 46-62.

Barber, B. K., and C. Buehler. "Family Cohesion and Enmeshment: Different Constructs, Different Effects." *Journal of Marriage and the Family* 58 (1996): 433-441.

Bartle, S. E., and R. M. Sabatelli. "Family System Dynamics, Identity Development, and Adolescent Alcohol Use: Implications for Family Treatment." *Family Relations* 38 (1989): 258-265.

Bassoff, E. S. "Mothering Adolescent Daughters: A Psychodynamic Perspective." *Journal of Counseling and Development* 65 (1987): 471-474.

Baumrind, D. "Current Patterns of Parental Authority." *Developmental Psychology.* Monograph 4, 1.2 (1971).

——. "Effective Parenting During the Early Adolescent Transition." *Advances in Family Research. Vol. 2, Family Transitions.* Ed. P. A. Cowan and E. M. Hetherington. Hillsdale: Erlbaum, 1991. 111-163.

——. "The Influence of Parenting Style on Adolescent Competence and Substance Abuse." *Journal of Early Adolescence* 11 (1991): 56-95.

Beavers, W. R. *Psychotherapy and Growth: A Family Systems Perspective.* New York: Brunner/Mazel, 1977.

——. *Successful Marriage: A Family Systems Approach to Couples Therapy.* New York: Norton, 1985.

Beman, D. S. "Risk Factors Leading to Adolescent Substance Abuse." *Adolescence* 30.117 (1995): 201-209.

Bernstein, A. C. "School-dazed." *Parents* 69 (1994): 87-88.

Blanchard, K., and S. Johnson. *The One Minute Manager.* New York: Morrow, 1982.

Blankenhorn, D. "Life Without Father." *USA Weekend* 24-26 Feb. 1995: 6-7.

Boss, P. "Normative Family Stress: Family Boundary Changes Across the Life-span." *Family Relations* 29 (1980): 445-450.

Bratter, B. I., C. J. Bratter, and T. E. Bratter. "Beyond Reality: The Need to (Re)gain Self-respect." *Psychotherapy* 32.1 (1995): 59-69.

Bronstein, P., et al. "Family and Parenting Behaviors Predicting Middle School Adjustment: A Longitudinal Study." *Family Relations* 45 (1996): 415-426.

Brooks-Gunn, J., and M. Zahaykevich. "Parent-Daughter Relationships in Early Adolescence: A Developmental Perspective." *Family Systems and Life-span Development.* Ed. K. Kreppner and R. M. Lerner. Hillsdale: Erlbaum, 1989. 223-246.

Brown, J. C., and L. Mann. "The Relationship Between Family Structure and Process Variables and Adolescent Decision Making." *Journal of Adolescence* 13 (1990): 25-37.

Brown, J. E., and L. Mann. "Effects of Family Structure and Parental Involvement on Adolescent Participation in Family Decisions." *Australian Journal of Sex, Marriage, and the Family* 9.2 (1988): 74-85.

Brown, L. "A Walk on the Wildlife Side: Destination Zambia." *Los Angeles Times* 23 Oct. 1994: L10-11.

Burt, M. *Stepfamilies Stepping Ahead: An Eight-Step Program for Successful Family Living.* Lincoln: Stepfamilies Press, 1989.

Butterfield, J. "Teens and Drinking: A Special Report." *USA Weekend* 12-14 Aug. 1994: 4-5.

Caissy, G. A. *Early Adolescence: Understanding the 10-15 Year Old.* New York: Plenum, 1994.

Carlson, B. W. "Uganda." *Los Angeles Times* 23 Oct. 1994: L11-13.

Carter, J. D. "Maturity: Psychological and Biblical." *Journal of Psychology and Theology* 5 (1974): 183-196.

Chused, J. F. "Interpretations and Their Consequences in Adolescence. Special Issue: Interpretation and Its Consequences." *Psychoanalytic Inquiry* 12.2 (1992): 275-295.

Clark, C. M. "Clinical Assessment of Adolescents Involved in Satanism." *Adolescence* 29.114 (1994): 461-468.

Clarke, J. I. *Self-Esteem: A Family Affair.* San Francisco: Harper, 1978.

Cloud, H. *When Your World Makes No Sense.* Nashville: Nelson, 1990.

Cloud, H., and J. Townsend. *Boundaries.* Grand Rapids: Zondervan, 1992.

———. *Boundaries for Kids.* Grand Rapids: Zondervan, 1988.

Coleman, L., et al., ed. *The NIV Serendipity Bible: 10th Anniversary Edition.* Grand Rapids: Zondervan, 1996.

Conger, J. J., and A. C. Peterson. *Adolescence and Youth.* New York: Harper and Row, 1984.

Cook, W. L., D. A. Kenny, and M. J. Goldstein. "Parental Affective Style Risk and the Family System: A Social Relations Model Analysis." *Journal of Abnormal Psychology* 100.4 (1991): 492-501.

Cooper, C. R., H. D. Grotevant, and S. M. Condon. "Individuality and Connectedness in the Family as a Context for Adolescent Identity Formation and Role Taking Skill." Ed. H. D. Grotevant and C. P. Cooper *Adolescent Development in the Family.* San Francisco: Jossey Bass, 1983. 43-49.

Cooper, J. *A primer of brief psychotherapy.* New York: Norton, 1995.

Coopersmith, S. *The Antecedents of Self-Esteem.* San Francisco: Freeman, 1967.

Cox, R. B., and W. A. Ray. "The Role of Theory in Treating Adolescent Substance Abuse." *Contemporary Family Therapy* 16.2 (1994): 131-144.

Demo, D. H., S. A. Small, and R. C. Savin-Williams. "Family Relations and the Self-Esteem of Adolescents and Their Parents." *Journal of Marriage and the Family* 49 (1987): 705-715.

Denton, R. E., and C. M. Kampfe. "The Relationship Between Family Variables and Adolescent Substance Abuse: A Literature Review." *Adolescence* 29.114 (1994): 475-495.

Deveaux, F. "Intergenerational Transmission of Cultural Family Patterns." *Family Therapy* 22.1 (1995): 17-23.

De Wilde, E. J., et al. "Social Support, Life Events, and Behavioral Characteristics of Psychologically Distressed Adolescents at High Risk for Attempting Suicide." *Adolescence* 29.113 (1994): 49-60.

Ellerbee, L. "Quitting Smoking Helps, but the After-Effects May Linger Forever." *San Bernardino Sun* 4 Feb. 1995: A7.

Evans, G. "Luann." Cartoon. *Los Angeles Times* 22 Feb. 1989: V5.

Field, T., et al. "Adolescents' Intimacy with Parents and Friends." *Adolescence* 30.117 (1995): 133-141.

Forehand, R., and S. Nousiainen. "Maternal and Paternal Parenting: Critical Dimensions in Adolescent Functioning." *Journal of Family Psychology* 7 (1993): 213-221.

Foxcroft, D. R., and G. Lowe. "Adolescent Drinking, Smoking and Other Substance Use Involvement: Links with Perceived Family Life." *Journal of Adolescence* 18 (1995): 159-177.

Ganguly, D. "Mother Teresa Forgives Producer of Documentary." *San Bernardino Sun* 13 Nov. 1994.

Gerlach, P. K. *Stepfamily in Formation!* 1997. Available: SAI, Inc., P.O. Box 3124, Oak Park, IL, 60303.

Getzoff, A., and C. McClenahan. *Stepkids: A Survival Guide for Teenagers in Stepfamilies and for Stepparents Doubtful of Their Own Survival.* New York: Walker, 1984.

Ginott, H. G. *Between Parent and Teenager.* New York: Avon, 1969.

Goleman, D. *Emotional Intelligence.* New York: Bantam, 1995.

Gottman, J. *Why Marriages Succeed or Fail.* New York: Simon and Schuster, 1994.

———. *The Heart of Parenting: Raising an Emotionally Intelligent Child.* New York: Simon and Schuster, 1997.

Granberg, L. I. *The Zondervan Encyclopedia of the Bible.* Vol. H-L. Ed. M. C. Tenney. Grand Rapids: Zondervan, 1975.

Grotevant, H. D., and C. R. Cooper. "Individuation in Family Relationships." *Human Development* 29 (1986): 82-100.

Harris, A. B., and T. A. Harris. *Staying OK.* New York: Avon, 1985.

Hendrick, B. "Supportive Dads Are a Key to Success." *San Bernardino Sun* 13 Nov. 1994.

Henry, C. S., et al. "Adolescent Suicide and Families: An Ecological Approach." *Family Therapy* 21.1 (1994): 63-80.

Hoopes, M. H., and J. M. Harper. *Birth Order Roles and Sibling Patterns in Individual and Family Therapy.* Rockville: Aspen, 1987.

Issler, K., and R. Habermaus. *How We Learn: A Christian Teacher's Guide to Educational Psychology.* Grand Rapids: Baker, 1994.

Jantz, G. *Hope, Help, and Healing for Eating Disorders.* Wheaton: Harold Shaw, 1995.

Johnson, A. M. "A Heritage Reclaimed." *Los Angeles Times* 23 Oct. 1994: L16-19.

Kafka, R. R., and P. London. "Communication in Relationships and Adolescent Substance Use: The Influence of Parents and Friends." *Adolescence* 26.103 (1991): 587-598.

Kaplan, L. J. *Adolescence: The Farewell to Childhood.* New York: Simon and Schuster, 1984.

Kempler, W. *Principles of Gestalt Family Therapy.* Costa Mesa: The Kempler Institute, 1974.

———. *Experiential Psychotherapy Within Families.* New York: Brunner/Mazel, 1981.

Klein, A. *The Healing Power of Humor.* Los Angeles: Tarcher, 1989.

Klein, K., et al. "Delinquency During the Transitions to Early Adulthood: Family and Parenting Predictors from Early Adolescence." *Adolescence* 32.125 (1997): 71-79.

Kohlberg, L., and C. Gilligan. "The Adolescent as Philosopher: The Discovery of the Self in a Post-Conventional World." *Daedalus* 100 (1971): 1051-1086.

Koopmans, M. "A Case of Family Dysfunction and Teenage Suicide Attempt: Applicability of a Family Systems Paradigm." *Adolescence* 30.117 (1995): 87-94.

Kubany, E. S., et al. "Verbalized Anger and Accusatory 'You' Messages as Cues for Anger and Antagonism Among Adolescents." *Adolescence* 27.107 (1992): 505-516.

La Coste, L. D., E. J. Ginter, and G. Whipple. "Intrafamily Communication and Familial Environment." *Psychological Reports* 61 (1987): 115-118.

Lazare, A. "Go Ahead Say You're Sorry." *Psychology Today* Jan.-Feb. 1995: 40-78.

Leek, F. "Shared Parenting Support Program: A Therapeutic Approach to Post-Divorce Co-Parenting." *The California Therapist* Jul-Aug. 1998: 52-54.

Lerner, R. M., and C. K. Olson. "The Imaginary Audience." *Parents* Feb. 1994: 133-134.

MacDonald, G. "Raising Teens to Make Right Choices." *Parents and Teenagers.* Ed. J. Kessler. Wheaton: Victor, 1984. 454.

Marett, K. M., D. H. Sprenkle, and R. A. Lewis. "Family Members' Perceptions of Family Boundaries and Their Relationship to Family Problems." *Family Therapy* 19.3 (1992): 233-242.

Masselam, V. S., R. F. Marcus, and C. L. Stunkard. "Parent-Adolescent Communication, Family Functioning, and School Performance." *Adolescence* 25.99 (1990): 725-737.

McDaniel, S. H., J. Hepworth, and W. J. Doherty. "Commentary: Medical Family Therapy with Somaticizing Patients: The Co-Creation of Therapeutic Stories." *Family Process, Inc.* 34 (1995): 349-361.

McFarland, B., and T. Baker-Baumann. *Feeding the Empty Heart.* Center City: Hazelden, 1988.

McOartland, G. "Betterways." *Bottom Line* 15 Aug. 1994: 9-10.

Middleton-Moz, J. *Children of Trauma.* Deerfield Beach: Health Communications, 1989.

Miller, A. *Prisoners of Childhood: The Drama of the Gifted Child and the Search for the True Self.* New York: Basic Books, 1987.

——. *Banished Knowledge: Facing Childhood Injuries.* New York: Doubleday, 1988.

Miller, K. E., et al. "Suicidal Adolescents' Perceptions of Their Family Environment." *Suicide and Life Threatening Behavior* 22.2 (1992): 226-239.

Miller, P. H. *Theories of Developmental Psychology.* San Francisco: W. H. Freeman, 1983.

Minirth, F., et al. *Love Hunger: Recovery from Food Addiction.* Nashville: Thomas Nelson, 1990.

Mitchell, C. E. "A Model for Forgiveness in Family Relationships." *Family Therapy* 22.1 (1995): 35-40.

Mitchell, J. *Anorexia.* Center City: Hazelden, 1985.

Moreno, A. B., and M. H. Thelen. "Eating Behavior in Junior High School Females." *Adolescence* 30.117 (1995): 171-174.

Necessary, J. R., and T. S. Parish. "Relationships of Parents' Perceived Actions Toward Their Children." *Adolescence* 30.117 (1995): 175-177.

Okie, S. "Teenage Chlamydia Cases Alarm Experts." *Los Angeles Times* 3 Sept. 1997: E2.

Papini, D. R. "Early Adolescent Age and Gender Differences in Patterns of Emotional Self-Disclosure to Parents and Friends." *Adolescence* 25.100 (1990): 959-976.

Papernow, P. L. "The Stepfamily Cycle: An Experiential Model of Stepfamily Development." *Family Relations* July 1984: 355-363. Available: 1910 West County Road B, Suite 147, St. Paul, MN 55113.

People Yearbook 1995: The Year in Review, 1994. New York: People Books.

Perry, J. M., R. W. Griggs, and R. Griggs. *The Road to Optimism.* San Ramon: Manfit Press, 1996.

Peterson, G. W., and B. C. Rollins. "Parent-Child Socialization as Symbolic Interaction." *Handbook of Marriage and the Family.* Ed. M. Sussman and S.

K. Steinmetz. New York: Plenum, 1987. 471-508.

Pipher, M. *Hunger Pains: The Modern Woman's Tragic Quest for Thinness.* New York: Ballantine, 1995.

——. *Reviving Ophelia: Saving the Selves of Adolescent Girls.* New York: Ballantine, 1994.

——. *The Shelter of Each Other: Rebuilding Our Families.* New York: Grosset/Putnam Book, 1996.

Pittman, F. *Turning Points: Treating Families in Transition and Crisis.* New York: Norton, 1987.

Popper, A. "I'm Me." *Parents* Feb. 1994: 98-100.

Ransom, D. C., and L. Fisher. "An Empirically Derived Typology of Families: II. Relationships with Adolescent Health." *Family Process, Inc.* 34 (1995): 183-197.

Reiss, D. and D. Klein. "Paradigms and Pathogenesis: A Family-Centered Approach to Problems of Etiology and Treatment of Psychiatric Disorders." *Family Interaction and Psychopathology: Theories, Methods, and Findings.* Ed. T. Jacob. New York: Plenum Press, 1987. 203-255.

Resnick, M. D., et al. "Protecting Adolescents from Harm." *JAMA* 278.10 (1997): 823-865.

Rodriguez, C. C. "Linking Golfers Around the World in Christ." *Links Letter.* 8.5 (1988): 1-6.

Scott, W. A., R. Scott, and M. McCabe. "Family Relationships and Children's Personality: A Cross-Cultural, Cross-Source Comparison." *British Journal of Social Psychology* 30.1 (1991): 1-20.

Siegel, J., and M. F. Shaughnessy. "There's a First Time for Everything: Understanding Adolescence." *Adolescence* 30.117 (1995): 217-221.

Starrels, M. E. "Gender Differences in Parent-Child Relations." *Journal of Family Issues* 15.1 (1994): 148-165.

Steinberg, L., and A. Levine. *You and Your Adolescent: A Parent's Guide for Ages 10 to 20.* New York: Harper and Row, 1990.

Stierlin, H. *Separating Parents and Adolescents.* New York: Aronson, 1981.

Szulc, T. "How to Talk to a Dictator." *Parade Magazine* 14 Sept. 1997: 6-8.

Tannen, D. *You Just Don't Understand.* New York: Ballantine, 1990.

Tesser, A. et al. "Conflict, the Role of Calm and Angry Parent-Child Discussion in Adolescent Adjustment." *Journal of Social and Clinical Psychology* 8.3 (1989): 317-330.

Tesser, A., and R. Forehand. "Adolescent Functioning: Communication and the Buffering of Parental Anger." *Journal of Social and Clinical Psychology* 10.2 (1992): 152-175.

Trad, P. V. "Adolescent Girls and Their Mothers: Realigning the Relationship." *The American Journal of Family Therapy* 23.1 (1995): 9-24.

Ullman, A. D., and A. Orenstein. "Why Some Children of Alcoholics Become Alcoholics: Emulation of the Drinker." *Adolescence* 29.113 (1994): 1-11.

VanVonderen, J. *Families Where Grace Is in Place.* Minneapolis: Bethany House, 1992.

Velligan, D. "Parental Communication Deviance: Its Relationship to Parent, Child, and Family System Variables." *Psychiatry Research* 26 (1988): 313-325.

Visher, E. B. and J. S. Visher. *Stepfamilies: Myths and Realities.* Seacaucus: The Citadel Press, 1979.

von Oech, R. *A Whack on the Side of the Head: How You Can Be More Creative.* New York: Warner Books, 1990.

Watzlawick, P. *The Situation Is Hopeless, but Not Serious.* New York: Norton, 1983.

Wexler, D. B. *The Prism Workbook: A Program for Innovative Self-Management.* New York: Norton, 1991.

White, M. *The Material Child: Coming of Age in Japan and America.* Los Angeles: University of California Press, 1994.

SUBJECT INDEX

Addiction, 157
Adjusting, 36, 38
Anger, 30, 71, 74, 78, 80
Attachment, 40
Attention, 18, 53-54, 125
Attitude, 35, 51, 66, 75-76, 99
Autonomy, 37, 39-40, 138, 141-45

Belonging, 51
Bonding, 36, 122
Boundaries
    between parents, 66
    flexible, 72-75
    healthy, 70-72
    intrusive, 66-70
    personal, 64-66

Coercion, 54-55
Communication, 36, 42-43, 90,
    100-1, 125
    Cross-cultural, 27-28
    Family, 44
Compliance, 60
Conflict, 78-79
Conflict Management, 80-81
Consequences, 60-61
Context, 144
Control, 53, 54-56
Culture, 22-23, 117, 139-40

Defensiveness, 100-1
Depression, 60, 68, 122, 168
Developmental Needs, 36-37

Eating Disorders
    Anorexia Nervosa, 174-75
    Bulimia, 176
    Obesity, 177
Emotional Intelligence, 124
Empathy, 56

Family
    decisions, 93
    healthy, 51-53
    patterns, 23-27, 28-30, 52-53
    secrets, 19, 30
    structure, 53-54
    warmth, 122-23, 124, 131
Flexibility, 72-75

Generations, 23-25, 28-29, 52-53
Grace, 69
Grudges, 87, 132-33

Humor, 70, 88, 111, 129-31,
    132-34, 139

Identity, 38, 149-51
Induction, 55-56

Laughter, 103-4, 127-28
Limits, 53-54, 56, 61, 65, 66, 88
Listening, 58-60, 105-7
Love Withdrawal, 55
Loyalty, 66-67, 82

Mistakes, 52

Modeling, 48-49, 66, 81-82, 99-100, 109-10

Negotiation
    apologies, 88-89, 94-95
    family, 91-92, 93, 95
    modeling, 81-82
    poor, 79-80
    positive, 80-81
    problem solving, 86-87
    strategies, 82-85, 89-91
Nurturance, 38, 56

Optimism, 43

Parenting
    authoritarian, 53-54, 60
    authoritative, 53-54
    permissive, 53-54
    rigid, 72-73, 169
    uninvolved, 53-54
Peer, 37, 155
Pessimism, 43
Play, 62-63
Power, 96-97, 102-3, 105-7
Projection, 49-51
Psychological myopia, 50

Rebellion, 33, 55, 100-1
Relaxation, 142, 143-44, 147
Rescuing, 40
Resentment, 24, 48, 60, 122, 132
Resistance, 55, 67, 83, 143
Respect, 97-99, 101-2

Satanism
    risk factors, 171
    stages, 172-73
Self-esteem, 43, 60-61, 151-52
Step-Parenting
    Child Paradox, 167
    Stages, 163-67
Stress, 38, 48, 66
Substance Abuse
    Alcohol, 122, 157
    Cigarettes, 22, 31
    Cocaine, 160
    Gypsum weed, 159
    Hallucinogens, 159
    Heroin, 161
    Inhalants, 158-59
    LSD, 159
    Marijuana, 157-58
    Methamphetamine, 159-60
    Peyote, 159
Success, 43
Suicide
    external risk factors, 168
    internal risk factors, 122, 168-70
Support, 53, 56-58, 60

Transitions, 36-37
Trust, 36, 69, 90

Understanding, 24, 33, 39, 132, 139
Unresolved issues, 23, 52, 122

Values, 108-9

Worldview, 32-33